"I was sold on *Every Day Is Saturday* as soon as I read the names of the chapters. From Grazing Platters to Cooking for Friends to Projects, Sarah describes my life— how I eat, who I eat with, and when I decide to hunker down in the kitchen for a while. The recipes are delicious and doable, and they take into account that we're busy. Our lives just needed to shift a little . . . to Saturday (even on a Wednesday!)."

CARLA HALL
author of *Carla Hall's Soul Food* and *Carla's Comfort Foods*

"I wanted to eat everything in this book and lick the pages clean. Sarah has created a book that is not only beautiful to look at, but also makes me want to start cooking and baking immediately."

CHRIS MOROCCO
Senior Editor, *Bon Appétit*

"At the heart of Sarah's book is a fundamental concept: simple is beautiful, and that applies to living as much as it does to cooking. She is the master of reminding us that, more than anything, food can be emotional sustenance, and her recipes are that jackpot combination of inspirational yet unbelievably approachable. Take it from someone who has been a longtime fan: this book is destined to be the most dog-eared cookbook on your shelf."

JENNY ROSENSTRACH
creator of *Dinner: A Love Story*

"In this timely, beautiful book, Sarah reminds us that we can bottle the magic of a Saturday night or Sunday supper with friends and family at a long table—where the flavors are bigger, wine flows a little more, and laughter grows a little louder—to nourish the ones we love any night of the week. All it takes is intention, a bit more planning, and her smart recipes as a roadmap to create big flavors with minor effort."

HUNTER LEWIS
Editor-in-Chief, *Food & Wine*

"*Every Day is Saturday* is all kinds of joy bundled up with the types of festive, vibrant recipes that make you feel like you can have it all, even on a crazy Tuesday."

MOLLY YEH
host of *Girl Meets Farm* and creator of *My Name Is Yeh*

"Everything Sarah cooks looks like something she's made expressly for your happiness. That she has two young children and a very busy life has always made me wonder, *How does she do it?* The answers are on each page of this book, which is as practical as it is beautiful. Sarah's get-ahead suggestions, her ideas for gathering—and pampering—people around the table, are down to earth. With Sarah at your side, every day will be Saturday in your home, too."

DORIE GREENSPAN
award-winning author of *Dorie's Cookies* and *Everyday Dorie*

EVERY D

IS

SATURD

Recipes + Strategies
for Easy Cooking,
Every Day of the Week

Sarah Copeland

photography by
Gentl + Hyers

CHRONICLE BOOKS
SAN FRANCISCO

Library of Congress Cataloging-in-Publication Data:

Names: Copeland, Sarah (Food expert) author.

Title: Every day is Saturday : recipes + strategies for easy cooking,
 every day of the week / by Sarah Copeland ; photographs by
 Gentl + Hyers.

Description: San Francisco : Chronicle Books, [2019] | Includes index.

Identifiers: LCCN 2018033082 | ISBN 9781452168524 (hardcover :
 alk. paper)

Subjects: LCSH: Cooking. | Quick and easy cooking. | LCGFT:
 Cookbooks.

Classification: LCC TX714 .C676 2019 | DDC 641.5—dc23
 LC record available at https://lccn.loc.gov/2018033082

Manufactured in China.

MIX
Paper from
responsible sources
FSC™ C008047
www.fsc.org

Prop styling by Sarah Copeland.

Food styling by Sarah Copeland.

Design by Vanessa Dina.

Typesetting by Frank Brayton.

10 9 8 7 6 5 4

Chronicle books and gifts are available at special quantity discounts to corpora-
tions, professional associations, literacy programs, and other organizations. For
details and discount information, please contact our premiums department at
corporatesales@chroniclebooks.com or at 1-800-759-0190.

Chronicle Books LLC
680 Second Street
San Francisco, California 94107
www.chroniclebooks.com

For András, Greta + Mátyás.
You are my Saturday, every day.

THINGS TO HAVE ON HAND
TO MAKE LIFE MORE DELICIOUS

Joy and ease in the kitchen come, mostly, from having a smart lineup of staples to pull from: foods you can grab and bring together into a thoughtful, flavorful meal, without a lot of time or effort. When your lineup is solid—and, as important, organized—preparing a meal doesn't have to start with list-making and a huge shop; it can happen on the fly. That's when good eating becomes a part of every day, *not* just for the weekend.

STEP 1: Kitchen Cleanse

Before you do anything else, get rid of anything that's taking up space but not serving you and your housemates well. Sometimes you have to toss old habits (and boxes and cans) to make room for new, more gratifying ones. Here's how:

1. Pull out your entire pantry (yes, all of it). Put things you use at least once a week on one section of your counter and things you use once or twice a month on the other section.

2. Get rid of anything past the expiration date. If it's close, make a plan to use that ingredient within a week, before it gets shuffled to the back of your pantry again. If you can't realistically make anything with it before it goes bad, part with it.

3. Donate anything you haven't cooked in the last six months, along with anything you tried but didn't enjoy. Sometimes things go off our rotation, and that's okay, but don't let them keep taking up space in your new, super-functional setup.

4. Invest in a set of clear containers—glass jars, Snapware, or anything else that fits your pantry and stacks neatly. (Small scoops are also helpful to keep inside jars of sugar, flour, oats, and any other oft-used pantry goods for quick use.)

5. Decant your most-used items into your new containers: bags of oats, grains, flours, sugar, cocoa, the rice you use most often, and so on. Make sure you can fit a whole bag of each item in each container—so you're not storing the jar *plus* a cup of leftovers in the bag.

6. Label everything clearly, with an expiration date.

7. Clean and wipe out the pantry, then restock the shelves, putting all your go-to's toward the front, and the lesser-used items toward the back, but where you can still see them.

8. Train everyone in the house in how the new system works. Make sure they're on board to update the grocery list (on a dry-erase, chalkboard, or paper pad kept at the ready) if they use up the last of something.

STEP 2: Get Stocked

This list of groceries will set you up for the kind of cooking you'll be doing in this book. Consider these the basics, the things you'll need to restock if you run out.

Grains and Breads
Rice: white, red, brown,
Arborio (for risotto), jasmine, basmati
Red or white quinoa
Rolled oats
All-purpose flour
All-purpose gluten-free flour (see page 14)
Whole-wheat flour or graham flour
Almond flour
Semolina flour
Cornmeal or polenta
Panko (Japanese bread crumbs)
Artisan whole-grain bread
Corn tortillas

Cans and Jars
Olives + capers
Cannellini + chickpeas
Dijon mustard + mayonnaise
White miso paste
Hot pepper paste (Asian, Italian,
or Hungarian)
Whole peeled tomatoes
Coconut milk
Peanut and/or almond butter
Tahini

Spices and Sweeteners
Coconut sugar and/or dark brown sugar
Granulated sugar (unrefined, unbleached)
Honey + maple syrup
Fine and flaky sea salt
Black peppercorns
Cinnamon (ground and sticks)
Coriander (ground)
Caraway and fennel seeds
Paprika
Vanilla extract and vanilla beans

Nuts and Seeds
Walnuts
Almonds
Pecans
Hazelnuts
Sunflower seeds
Pumpkin seeds
Sesame seeds
Poppy seeds

Cocoa and Chocolate
Bittersweet chocolate (70%)
Extra-large semisweet or bittersweet
chocolate chips
Dutch-processed (or alkalized)
cocoa powder

Oils and Vinegars
Extra-virgin olive oil
Coconut oil
Toasted sesame oil
Canola or grapeseed oil
White and red wine vinegar
Apple cider, white, and rice vinegar
Soy sauce or tamari

Produce
Fresh ginger
Garlic
White and red onions
Shallots
Lemons and limes
Fresh herbs, such as mint, dill, and chives

Dairy and Nondairy
Unsalted butter
Whole milk
Nut milk
Buttermilk
Plain, whole-milk yogurt
Eggs (large)
Ricotta, Parmesan, Manchego,
feta, and cotija cheese

These ingredients—some you may know and already buy, some you may not—can help next-level your everyday dinner game, and weekend feasting, too.

GLUTEN-FREE FLOUR

I keep both all-purpose and all-purpose gluten-free flour at home. Where I think the result is slightly superior for one flour over the other, I've listed that one first. Occasionally, something benefits from the lightness of gluten-free flour, and I actually prefer it. But all of the recipes in this book were tested with both, so you can choose what works best for your needs.

If you choose to bake with a gluten-free flour, look for Cup4Cup multipurpose gluten-free flour blend (in a blue pouch) or Bob's Red Mill Gluten Free 1-to-1 Baking Flour (in a cellophane bag with a blue label), both of which perform like standard white flour. Bob's Red Mill also makes a Gluten Free All Purpose Baking Flour made with chickpea flour (in a cellophane bag with a red label); avoid this flour in these recipes, as the chickpea lends a strong earthy taste to sweets and baked goods.

ALMOND FLOUR

Almond flour makes everything taste better: nuttier, richer, and more toothsome. I frequently use it for baking because I love that it adds flavor, fiber, and vitamins to everything from cookies to cakes. You can find it in everyday supermarkets (check the gluten-free or health food aisles) or buy it in bulk online, as I do. Store excess in the refrigerator or freezer, where it lasts longer. Obviously, this flour is out for you if someone in your family has a nut allergy; substitute white flour, such as all-purpose or gluten-free flour instead, or use graham flour for a nuttier flavor and a nutrient boost.

CASTELVETRANO OLIVES

These plump, meaty green olives are an utter treat. Eat them alone, alongside charcuterie, or pit and tear or chop them into salads. They are also delicious baked alongside chicken with lemons and olive oil (page 136). They're widely available in good grocery stores at the olive deli bar, but when I find them in the jar I buy three jars at a time so we never run out.

FINE SEA SALT

Many chefs use kosher salt for cooking. It's easy to control and requires arguably less. But I'm not sold. Why? Simple: I trust something harvested from nature since ancient times more than a salt manufactured by man (sorry, kosher). Sea salt is *the* original salt, and it's never let me down. I use fine sea salt for basic cooking *and* baking (a one-size-fits-all salt) and Maldon flaky sea salt (see facing page) for nuanced seasoning. Yes, it's more expensive than kosher or iodized (table salt), but only a tiny bit; you can find it for less than $5 a pound at Trader Joe's, Costco, and Sam's Club—as well as online—and a pound will last you a long, long time. It doesn't really matter what kind you buy: Celtic, Dead Sea, Mediterranean, or even Himalayan (which isn't from the sea, but like sea salt is pure and full of valuable trace minerals). Kosher *will* work in these recipes (you may need about 25 percent more), as will iodized table salt (which is a one-for-one conversion with fine sea salt).

Here's what's most important: Pick a salt and stick with it so you learn how to control it, and taste early and often while cooking, so you don't over- or underseason your food.

MALDON SEA SALT

This flaky, hand-harvested sea salt is a crowd favorite for finishing salads, steaks, fish, roasted vegetables, avocado, and just about anything. The diamond-shaped flakes of Maldon hit your palate and then melt on your tongue, which means you need a *lot* less salt for something to taste amazing.

If you have it, you can also use *fleur de sel*, a delicate coarse sea salt, which can be pricier but is also delicious, any time I call for Maldon.

COCONUT SUGAR AND UNREFINED SUGAR

Sugar is sugar, but I always prefer the most natural kind—like coconut sugar instead of brown sugar, and unrefined, unbleached organic sugar instead of standard granulated. It makes me feel more relaxed about the sweets I offer my family. In this book I use coconut sugar interchangeably with dark *or* light brown sugar. All the baked goods were tested with standard sugars and these alternatives, so whichever you have and use most often will work. Baking at home is already better for you than anything in a box, and will reward you with a lifetime of good memories.

DAIRY

All the dairy used in this book is whole milk (full fat, not skimmed) and plain (no vanilla or sweeteners added). If all you have at home is reduced-fat milk or low-fat yogurt, expect slightly less robust results. I also always buy organic milk, eggs, and butter when I can.

Do watch out for sweeteners or vanilla flavoring in yogurt or nut milks; it can impart a strong flavor. Skip them if you're trying to make something savory. For any nondairy substitutes (nut milk, oat milk, rice milk, soy milk, and so on), unsweetened is best for controlling sugar.

COTIJA CHEESE

This super-salty, crumbly Mexican cheese adds oodles of flavor to Mexican soups like pozole (page 82) or All-Season Chicken Soup with Tortillas and Avocado (page 113). It's too salty to eat plain, but it grates beautiful snowy flakes that melt into warm soups and give each bite an irresistible flavor. If you can't find it (in the dairy or international aisle at the supermarket or a Mexican grocery store), ricotta salata is a close second.

TAHINI

Tahini, a thick butter of toasted ground sesame seeds, is the secret ingredient in hummus, halva, and many other Middle Eastern favorites. Check the expiration date before buying—it can turn rancid if old. Keep it fresh longer in the refrigerator; bring to room temperature and stir well before using.

BREAKF
BRUNCI

MIGHTY YOGURT BOWLS WITH CURRANTS AND PEACHES

PREP TIME: **5 MINUTES**

TOTAL TIME: **5 MINUTES** OR **OVERNIGHT**

SERVES **4**

Quick-to-make chia pudding, with the right touch, can turn an everyday yogurt bowl into something beautiful and irresistibly creamy. The secret is to keep the chia mixture loose, and treat it like a condiment, rather than the main event. (Chia thickens as it sets in liquid, so you'll need to add fewer seeds if you plan to let it sit overnight.) Serve this creamy, coconut-milk goodness with loads of fresh fruit, as a quick morning breakfast bowl that's nearly ready to go when you wake up.

¾ cup (180 ml) whole milk, or almond, coconut, or hazelnut milk

2 to 3 tsp pure maple syrup

1 tsp pure vanilla extract

2 to 3 Tbsp chia seeds

Plain yogurt, for serving

Currants, peaches, berries, honey, or maple syrup, for topping

Combine the milk, maple syrup, vanilla, and 2 table-spoons chia seeds in a mason jar or any glass container with a tight-fitting lid. Give it a shake or a stir and refrigerate up to overnight, or stir in the remaining chia to thicken if you plan to use right away. Spoon the chia mixture over yogurt, and top with fresh fruit and honey or maple syrup.

TOASTED MANY-SEED MUESLI WITH SUMMER FRUITS

PREP TIME: **5 MINUTES**

TOTAL TIME: **30 MINUTES**

SERVES **8**
(makes 8½ cups/830 g)

Muesli answers the call for an ideal weekday breakfast. It's easy, sustaining, and delicious, and it works in any season.

There are two kinds of muesli: The first is the thickened pudding-like muesli of grains and fruits soaked in milk overnight, which I adore, but makes my husband and kids balk (if you've traveled to Austria, Switzerland, or Germany, you've probably had this). The other, the kind we eat most days, is a bit more like a homemade cold cereal, served on the fly with a splash of milk or yogurt. This recipe works either way.

The best way to fall in love with muesli is to only add the ingredients *you* love. I serve muesli with almost any fruit, from watermelon (a revelation!) to peaches to cherries and berries, currants, pears, grated apple, and even dried fruit.

6 cups (600 g) old-fashioned rolled oats

1 cup (about 120 g) almonds, walnuts, or pistachios, roughly chopped

⅓ cup (80 ml) pure maple syrup

¼ cup (60 ml) olive, coconut, or sesame oil

¼ cup (35 g) poppy seeds

¼ cup (35 g) sunflower seeds

¼ cup (35 g) sesame seeds (black or white)

2 tsp pure vanilla extract

1 tsp fine sea salt

¼ tsp ground ginger (optional)

FOR SERVING

Milk, plain yogurt, or a nondairy substitute

Chopped fruit, such as plums, figs, cherries, peaches, watermelon, apples, and pears

Preheat the oven to 350°F (175°C). Combine the oats, nuts, maple syrup, oil, poppy seeds, sunflower seeds, sesame seeds, vanilla, salt, and ginger (if using) in a large bowl. Transfer to two rimmed baking sheets. Bake, stirring, until golden brown, 18 to 24 minutes.

cont'd

Serve the muesli with milk, yogurt, or both, topped with fruit, or stir together and soak from 1 hour up to overnight in the refrigerator.

GOOD TO KNOW

For the oil in this recipe, you can use olive oil, coconut oil, or sesame oil, depending on what flavor you love. Toasted sesame oil has become my favorite, a beautifully earthy undertone for all the soft flavors of milk and fruits.

GET AHEAD

Make the dry muesli in advance and store in an airtight container at room temperature for up to 2 weeks, or the freezer for up to 1 month. To make a full ready-to-go breakfast, stir all your ingredients, including toppings, together in a bowl or to-go container. Cover and refrigerate overnight; serve cold or at room temperature.

CHEATER'S MUESLI

We don't do a lot of boxed cereal at home, so my kids look forward to heaping bowls of it on visits to my parents, where my dad stocks the classics, like Frosted Mini-Wheats. At first I fought him on it, until one day I added a handful of chia seeds, some sunflower seeds, blueberries, and peach slices to their bowls, and discovered a compromise I can get behind. We call it Cheater's Muesli, or Duke's Mixture (my dad's term), and everyone's on board.

Growing up, waffles were a special-occasion treat, the kind of breakfast that made my mom sigh (waffle iron, batter spills, over-sugared kids) and my dad smile with glee (strawberries, whipped cream, truly living). In this way, my marriage is similar: I am for a simpler, saner, healthier morning. András is for waffles. Always for waffles.

Just like my mom, my solution is making him our resident waffle chef. For as many Sundays as I can remember he's pulled out the Belgian waffle iron and stood at the counter with the kids mixing milk and eggs and flour into batter.

In the end I couldn't resist joining in, tweaking our go-to waffle into something lighter, but still wholesome and sustaining. What emerged is an easy waffle that's crispy outside, airy and moist inside, and every bit good for you while still tasting like that old favorite from weekends as a kid. (Bonus: It can be easily made both gluten and dairy free.)

Our waffle isn't *the family waffle* unless it's loaded to the nines with yogurt (instead of whipped cream), berries, fried eggs, and maple syrup. Sounds crazy, right? But trust me, the maple and egg yolk mingle, and it's so very good.

1½ cups (235 g) gluten-free flour blend or (210 g) all-purpose flour

3 Tbsp cooked quinoa, cooled

2 Tbsp chia seeds

2 tsp unrefined cane sugar

1½ tsp baking powder

½ tsp fine sea salt

1½ cups (360 ml) unsweetened almond milk

½ cup (120 ml) vegetable oil, plus more for the waffle iron

2 large eggs, lightly beaten

1 tsp pure vanilla extract

Plain yogurt (optional) and fresh berries (or any fruit), for serving

4 eggs, fried, for serving (optional)

Pure maple syrup, for serving

cont'd

THE FAMILY WAFFLE

PREP TIME: **10 MINUTES**

TOTAL TIME: **40 MINUTES**

SERVES **4**
(makes 4 Belgian waffles or 8 thin waffles)

Preheat a waffle iron (we like a Belgian waffle maker, but any will work). Whisk together the flour, quinoa, chia seeds, sugar, baking powder, and salt. In a separate bowl, whisk together the almond milk, oil, eggs, and vanilla. When your waffle iron is hot and ready to use, stir the milk mixture into the flour mixture until just combined; the batter will be loose, the consistency of heavy cream.

Spray or brush the waffle iron very lightly with oil. (If your waffle iron is seasoned or nonstick, you should only need to do this once before you begin, not between every waffle, which makes them taste greasy.) Ladle 1 heaping cup (240 ml) of the batter into the waffle iron and cook until golden brown, 12 to 14 minutes. Set aside on a rack while you cook the remaining waffles to keep them crispy (stacking will make them steam and get soggy). Serve the waffles warm with berries, a dollop of yogurt or a fried egg (if desired), and a drizzle of maple syrup, or anything else you desire.

GET AHEAD

Keep prepared batter in the refrigerator, covered, up to overnight. Or bake the waffles, cool, and freeze them in batches of two in large resealable freezer bags. To eat, bring to room temperature for 5 to 10 minutes, and toast to warm through. If you are making them fresh to order, you should know—as my kids and guests do—that waffle cooking is a one-by-one affair; everyone is allowed to eat their waffle hot and fresh off the press, when they're best, while the rest cook. If you want many waffles hot and ready at once, see Go Big, facing page.

Go Big

This recipe doubles easily. Keep the waffles warm on a sheet pan with a rack, in a preheated 325°F (165°C) oven, while you cook the remaining waffles.

Really, Quinoa?

Yes. Keep extra cooked in sealed containers in the freezer. If you *don't* have already cooked quinoa, skip it. You may miss the signature quinoa freckles, but the chia adds texture and nutrients.

What If I'm Not Gluten Free?

Gluten-free flour makes these lighter, but they work beautifully with all-purpose white flour, too.

No Milk?

You can count on these for a dairy-free but decadent breakfast, but it's fine to substitute whole milk instead.

Scandi Style

For thin and crisp, Scandinavian-style waffles, use only ½ cup (120 ml) batter for each, and cook for 6 to 8 minutes.

Johnny cakes are an addictive southern specialty, set apart from regular pancakes for their texture and taste. Their corn flavor is hard to mistake, making them a perfect backdrop for butter and maple syrup. My family especially loves them with a bit of tangy, juicy summer fruit on top: rhubarb, lightly steeped in maple syrup and tossed with sour cherries or raspberries.

These aren't textbook Johnny cakes, but this recipe makes utterly gorgeous pancakes and is still easy enough to make on repeat every weekend.

JOHNNY CAKES WITH RHUBARB AND SOUR CHERRIES

PREP TIME: **10 MINUTES**

TOTAL TIME: **20 MINUTES**

SERVES **4**
(makes 8 large pancakes)

TOPPING

2 thick stalks ruby red rhubarb, sliced on the bias (about 2 cups/200 g)

¼ cup (60 ml) pure maple syrup, plus more for serving

One 24-oz (680-g) jar pitted sour cherries, in syrup or juices

PANCAKES

1 cup (140 g) fine to medium cornmeal

1 cup (140 g) all-purpose flour or (155 g) gluten-free flour

1 Tbsp sugar

1 tsp baking soda

¼ tsp fine sea salt

1 large egg, lightly beaten

1⅓ cups (320 ml) buttermilk

4 Tbsp (½ stick) unsalted butter, melted, plus more for cooking

Plain yogurt, for serving

TO MAKE THE TOPPING: Combine the rhubarb and maple syrup in a medium pot with a tight-fitting lid. Cook over medium-low heat until the syrup bubbles just slightly and the rhubarb is steaming, but not breaking down, 1 to 2 minutes. Remove from the heat, cover, and let the rhubarb sit in the syrup until it softens but is still holding its shape and bright red in color. Toss with the cherries and just enough of the cherry juices to turn the syrup red, but still leave it

cont'd

When it comes to breakfast, there ar[e]
moms: those who put chocolate chips [in]
pancakes and those who don't. I'm a [____]
of mom. My sister is a chocolate chip [____]
Her chocolate chip pancakes have us [____]
and soul.

My kids don't have *any* shortage [____]
wit: visit the sweets chapter); betwee[n]
holidays and my baking addiction, the[____]
deprived. But sometimes I want to be [____]
chips at breakfast kind of mom. For t[____]
these pancakes.

It would be unfair to call these [____]
indulgent or healthy—they are a littl[e]
Most of all, these pancakes are a fee[____]
when I've made them. They're about [____]
kind of mom, if only once in a while.

1 ripe banana

1 tsp pure vanilla extract

¾ cup (180 ml) whole milk or almon[d]

½ cup (70 g) buckwheat flour

½ cup (50 g) quick-cooking or plain [____]
(not thick)

1 tsp baking powder

1 Tbsp sugar

½ tsp fine sea salt

Unsalted butter or coconut oil

Scant ½ cup (about 80 g) bitterswe[et]
chips

Honey, pure maple syrup, or powde[red]
serving

Smash the banana with a fork into a [____]
(don't be tempted to add the other [____]
before this is done). Add the vanilla [____]
mash together. In a separate bowl, [whisk]
buckwheat flour, oats, baking powde[r]
Add the wet to the dry ingredients [____]
being careful not to overmix; you wa[nt]
pancakes light and airy. Too much st[____]
them gummy and dense.

Heat a cast-iron griddle or skillet over medium heat until evenly warm. Add a bit of butter to coat the surface. When the butter sizzles, drop a scant ¼ cup (60 ml) of batter onto the skillet in batches, leaving 2 inches (5 cm) between the pancakes. (Don't make your pancakes big; they are tender because there's no egg to bind the batter.) Cook until just starting to bubble around the edges. Dot the pancakes with chocolate chips, then flip (they should release easily from the griddle). Cook on the second side until just done, usually a minute or two (if the pancake stays on the heat too long, the chocolate will scorch), turning the heat to low if needed. Repeat until all the batter is used. Serve warm with butter and honey.

GET AHEAD

Combine all the wet ingredients, and all the dry ingredients, and store separately in the refrigerator overnight. Stir the wet and dry together in the morning while you preheat the griddle.

DOUBLE UP

I always make two batches of these, but they are most tender when I mix up one batch at a time, start cooking them, then repeat, so I've given you a single batch here.

BUCKWHEAT FLOUR

Chances are your regular grocery store will only carry one kind of buckwheat flour, and whatever kind you get will work, but flours from different brands yield slightly different results. If your buckwheat flour seems coarse, and flecked with dark gray bits, you'll get slightly darker pancakes (it's what I used for the photo, and what I prefer). Buckwheat flour can also be labeled *light*, which is finer, a subtle gray color, and yields a more delicate pancake. It can also lend an odd greenish hue, but they still taste delicious. My family never complains.

GOOD TO KNOW

For the fluffiest, most tender pancakes, you want *just enou* liquid. Too little makes panc and dense; too much yields tough-tasting cake. Watch f batter to just come together bubble up a bit as it sits (a of the buttermilk and baking Start with slightly less liquid is called for, especially if usi gluten-free flour, which tenc soak up less moisture. Cook first pancake, and if it's not liking, stir in a tablespoon or more buttermilk, or even wa the batter feels just right.

SCRAMBLED EGGS WITH AVOCADO, PEA SHOOTS, AND SESAME SEEDS

PREP TIME: **5 MINUTES**

TOTAL TIME: **5 MINUTES**

SERVES **4**

This five-minute breakfast feels both healthy and indulgent. It requires no prep but has a delicious, vibrant reward that lasts until lunchtime. I learned to make scrambled eggs while cooking in French restaurants, where we ate them often for family meal any time of day (an alluring alternative to the other frequent and economical offerings of plain buttered pasta or tripe stew). Whisk or stir them constantly over very low heat, and the eggs become almost custardy, barely set and silky. Scoop them onto thin toast, or spoon into your mouth with avocado and hot sauce and enjoy in all their luscious glory.

1 Tbsp extra-virgin olive oil, plus more for drizzling

8 eggs, beaten

Toast

1 large ripe avocado, sliced

1 heaping handful of pea shoots

Black sesame seeds, for serving

1 lemon or lime, cut into wedges

Coarse sea salt, such as Maldon

Hot sauce or sriracha, for serving

Heat the oil in a medium nonstick or regular skillet over medium-low heat. Add the eggs and let them set to cook a bit, about 40 seconds. Use a heatproof spatula to scoot the eggs across the pan, back and forth, to cook into medium curds. For smaller curds (and the creamiest eggs), use a whisk, moving the eggs constantly over low heat until the eggs are lightly cooked but still pale and creamy, just shy of runny (if you can smell a cooked egg aroma in the air, they've gone too far).

Serve with toast on a plate or shallow bowl, with avocado, pea shoots, and sesame seeds. Squeeze the lemon over the top, sprinkle with salt, and drizzle with more oil, hot sauce, or anything else you desire.

Add Heat

Avocado halves or quarters are
perfect vessels for smoked hot
sauce, sriracha, or anything else
that heats up your morning.

Power Up

Get green power early with
pea shoots, microgreens, or
spicy arugula on the side. Drizzle
greens and avocado with lemon.

On Point

Serve with toasted bread
or English muffins, lavished
with oil or butter.

I know you don't need a recipe for fruit salad, but a reminder to make it more often never hurts. And this isn't your ordinary fruit salad. If made right, it should conjure your happiest vacation days. For me, it's a summer trip to Maui with my parents, my husband, and our kids. Though there was plenty of chasing a toddler down beaches and splashing through pools, never turning your head for a second, there was also infinite sunshine, laughter, downy feather pillows, and many, many generous fruit plates that seemed to make themselves and never run out—which is relaxation itself.

When I want to bring back Hawaii, and quick, this is what I make. Give yourself that vacation breakfast feeling some mornings. Don't skip the lime and salt, which elevate the fruit, and bring vacationland front and center to your plate.

VACATION FRUIT SALAD

TOTAL TIME: **10 MINUTES**

SERVES **4**

1 seedless watermelon, rind removed

1 papaya or cantaloupe, rind and seeds removed

Strawberries, cherries, blackberries, or raspberries, rinsed

2 limes, halved

Fresh lemon verbena leaves or toasted coconut, for serving

Flaky sea salt, such as Maldon, for serving

Cut the melon into large triangles and arrange on the plate. Scoop the papaya into balls using a melon baller or small ice cream scoop (save the trimmings for smoothies). Arrange the fruit in a shallow bowl and squeeze lime juice all over. Sprinkle with lemon verbena and salt (making sure it hits the watermelon in a few spots), and indulge.

cont'd

GET AHEAD

Most of these fruits can be trimmed, seeded, and cut into shapes a night or two before (and the limes halved). For the ultimate luxury, cut enough for seconds, and store the fruits for the next day (separately) in tightly sealed containers. Compose your salad fresh in the morning, and add the lime, lemon verbena, and salt just before eating.

Nutritionally speaking, most muffins are cupcakes, disguised as breakfast. I set out to make a muffin that wasn't. I baked muffins with every kind of flour under the sun. I creamed butter. I melted butter. I tried coconut oil, olive oil, canola oil. My family ate about a hundred muffins each, and they were all very good.

After eating a hundred healthy-ish muffins, I realized what we all *really* wanted was the kind of muffin my mom had waiting for us on special Sundays, with wild blueberries that streaked the tender crumb with deep bursts of blue. A muffin so good that a thick pat of butter could only improve it, but one that didn't really *need* butter at all.

This muffin isn't healthy, or really even healthy-ish (although, as my daughter reminds me, blueberries are healthy!), but they are ethereal and lovely and infinitely repeatable. I make them for the first day of school, the swim team party, weekend guests, and sleepovers—and enjoy them totally guilt free.

½ cup (1 stick) unsalted butter, at room temperature

1 tsp grated lemon zest or freshly grated ginger (your choice)

1 cup (200 g) unbleached sugar

2 large eggs, at room temperature

2 cups (280 g) all-purpose or (310 g) gluten-free flour

2 tsp baking powder

½ tsp fine sea salt

½ cup (120 ml) buttermilk

1½ cups (210 g) fresh or frozen blueberries

Coarse sugar, for sprinkling

Cold unsalted butter and Maldon salt, for serving

Preheat the oven to 375°F (190°C) and line two 6-cup muffin pans with paper cupcake liners.

Cream the butter, lemon zest, and unbleached sugar in a large bowl until light and fluffy, a full 5 minutes. Add the eggs one at a time, beating well after each addition.

cont'd

NOSTALGIA-WINS BLUEBERRY MUFFINS

PREP TIME: **20 MINUTES**

TOTAL TIME: **50 MINUTES**

MAKES **12 MUFFINS**

In a separate bowl, whisk together the flour, baking powder, and salt. Spoon about half of the flour mixture into the butter mixture, followed by half of the buttermilk; mix until smooth. Repeat with the remaining flour and buttermilk, and mix, being careful not to overmix.

Crush half the blueberries lightly with a fork (they should look broken and a little juicy, but not evenly smashed) and fold them loosely into the batter so that it streaks the batter lightly (without giving it an overall blue hue). Gently fold in the remaining berries with a few turns of the spatula, and scoop ⅓ cup (80 ml) into each well of the prepared muffin tins.

Sprinkle with coarse sugar and bake until the muffins just spring back when pressed lightly, 30 to 35 minutes. Set on a wire rack to cool for 5 to 10 minutes, and serve warm with butter and Maldon salt.

GET AHEAD
These muffins are worth waking up a little earlier for because they taste absolutely best baked right before eating. But do like a chef and prep your ingredients up to two days before: Combine all the wet ingredients, and all the dry ingredients, and store separately in the refrigerator overnight. Stir the wet and dry together in the morning while you preheat the oven.

GOOD TO KNOW
To make mini muffins, bake for 20 minutes. Makes 24.

This is a quick breakfast I could eat every weekday that satisfies like no boxed cereal or packaged oatmeal ever could. First, because it's hearty and warm, and second because it's downright delicious. The creamy blend of oats and polenta, with pops of warm plumped raisins and soft bananas, sends you off into a cold or rainy day with that good feeling that you've already treated yourself. Don't skip the sea salt—it brings the subtle sweetness to life.

1½ cups (150 g) rolled oats

½ cup (70 g) stone-ground polenta

½ tsp fine sea salt

½ cup (70 g) raisins

1 cup (240 ml) whole milk or almond or oat milk, plus more for serving

1 banana, halved lengthwise and sliced

Pure maple syrup, brown sugar, or honey, for serving

Combine the oats, polenta, 5 cups (1.2 L) water, the salt, and raisins in a saucepan and bring to a boil. Cook over medium-low heat, stirring occasionally (both grains will suck up water and make the mixture stick if you don't stir), until the polenta is al dente, about 10 minutes. Add the milk and banana, and continue cooking over low heat, stirring from time to time, until just tender and creamy, 5 minutes more, adding more milk if desired. Serve warm, with maple syrup for drizzling.

cont'd

HOT OATS AND POLENTA WITH RAISINS AND BANANAS

PREP TIME: **5 MINUTES**

TOTAL TIME: **20 MINUTES**

SERVES **4**

GET AHEAD

Combine the oats, polenta, water, and salt before you go to bed, to reduce the cooking time by almost half. In the morning, start cooking as directed, adding the raisins, milk, and bananas 5 minutes into cooking. Continue cooking until creamy, about 5 minutes more.

CORNMEAL V. POLENTA

Cornmeal and polenta are often labeled interchangeably. Look for stone-ground polenta or cornmeal, which has a better texture. Skip anything labeled coarse (it will take too long to cook) or fine cornmeal (which can be pasty). While not as hearty and delicious, quick-cooking oats and polenta also work here, and will reduce the overall cooking time by 5 minutes.

LEFTOVER BROWN RICE BREAKFAST PORRIDGE

PREP TIME: **5 MINUTES**

TOTAL TIME: **20 MINUTES**

SERVES **4**

If you're making rice for dinner, err on the too-much side, and here's why: a small pot and some milk can transform leftover rice into a warm spoonable cereal in no time, the kind my family craves all fall and winter long.

We season it with a cinnamon stick (or a pinch of ground cinnamon, if that's what you have) and vanilla, but no sweeteners; rice and milk have their own subtle sweetness. A drizzle of honey, maple syrup, or cinnamon sugar at the end, plus berries or other favorite fruits, is all you need. On bitterly cold days, or just any day we need an extra sustaining power, I think like a farm girl and drizzle the hot porridge with fresh cream. The breakfast table is always quiet those mornings, save for the satisfied slurps of happy customers.

3 cups (540 g) leftover cooked brown or white rice (or a mixture)

3 cups (720 ml) whole milk or almond, hazelnut, oat, or rice milk, plus more for serving

1 small cinnamon stick

½ tsp pure vanilla extract

½ tsp fine sea salt

Flaky sea salt, such as Maldon, for serving (optional)

Honey, pure maple syrup, or cinnamon sugar, for serving

Berries, for serving

Heat the rice, milk, cinnamon, vanilla, and fine salt in a saucepan over medium heat until warmed through, 5 to 10 minutes. Continue cooking at a low simmer until the milk thickens and the rice breaks down just slightly, about 5 minutes more. Remove the cinnamon stick and serve warm, with a pinch of flaky salt (if using), honey, and berries.

THE HUNGRIEST HOUSEGUEST

I *love* a full house. When we first bought a house, after many years of living in the world's smallest apartment in New York City, we had a table for eight for the first time in my adult life. That year, I invited friends to stay almost every weekend. I loved all our raucous, late-night dinners, with wine and kids and music and laughter all thrown in the mix. Even more, I loved waking up under the same roof, and gathering again, still in pajamas, for the first meal of the day.

But feeding houseguests isn't for the meek; it takes planning and grace. Especially if one houseguest in particular isn't just hungry, he's *staaarving* (in his southern Missouri twang). He might be related to me.

My dad is an emphatic man. I love this about him. When my mom makes dinner, he'll smack and lick his lips wildly, saying, "Honey, honey, *honey*! This is delicious!" (It took me years to stop expecting everyone else to do the same.) He chips in to set the table, helps with the dishes, is a pro at feeding toddlers. In short: He's an ideal, jovial houseguest. But when he's hungry, nothing can curb his zeal for the next meal.

It's not his fault. My grandmother—his mother—was a legendary host who seemed to be able to do it all: raise six kids, put three hot meals on the table each day, and even go back to college, with her two youngest in tow. Well into her eighties, there were often twenty people under her roof for whole weekends at a time. I'd wake up when the sun was just starting to glow through the attic windows where I slept. Downstairs, I could hear her sausage patties snapping against the fat in a cast-iron pan, the smell of fresh biscuits and gravy wafting up the steep, narrow steps. I'd run down, eager to help, but the table was already laid with rose-patterned china, heaped high with biscuits, homemade jellies, and velvety scrambled eggs. In the kitchen, my grandfather would stand beside her, following orders while she stirred orange juice in her squat glass pitcher, with a pinch of sugar. It's how she served up all of life.

On my best days, I am like my grandma. Most days, though, I'm just human.

Enthusiasm for food runs in the family. To wit: my son, Mátyás. At three years old, his first words at 5 a.m. are "I'm hunnnnnnngry." He bursts into tears if he doesn't deem his portion as large as his father's. And if I take too long getting down to the kitchen, I might find him in his diaper in front of the refrigerator, raw zucchini in one hand and a fistful of berries in the other, eyeing the shelves for what to eat next.

Sigh.

Once, I had bounding toddler-like energy, too, but since I had kids, I've adopted my husband's groggy, pajama-clad saunter to the kitchen, what I now affectionately call *the slow start*. Trying to beat a hearty appetite to the punch every time is asking for a fail.

The fact is, feeding people—even people you love dearly—could be a chore. But it doesn't have to be. You could rise in the wee hours, as my grandmother did. You could get help from take-out or resort to less healthy, more filling foods. Or, like me, you might find the art of baiting your home with DIY offerings a bit more your style. Consider this your host-with-the-most free pass.

HOW TO FEED YOUR HUNGRIEST HOUSEGUESTS (WITHOUT LIFTING A WHISK)

+ Always keep fresh bread and butter in the house. Before you go to bed, set the bread (wrapped in a tea towel), a small dish of butter, and a jar of jelly with a spoon out on a tray on the kitchen counter for early risers. Keep a second, tightly wrapped loaf or two of bread in the freezer for emergencies.

+ Create a DIY muesli station with jars of muesli (page 22), dried fruit, a stack of bowls, and a mug filled with clean spoons. Leave a *Help yourself, milk and yogurt are in the fridge* note nearby to cue self-service.

+ Keep ample bowls of grab-and-go fruits like apples, bananas, pears, and clementines on the counter at the ready. Ditto jars of shelled nuts like cashews, pistachios, almonds, or walnuts.

+ Create an organized coffee and tea station (as simple as one drawer, fully stocked, with a stack of mugs nearby) in your house and give guests a full round-the-clock invitation to self-serve.

+ Stock jars of apple chips or dried fruit in living areas, where people can enjoy a healthy-ish nibble in private.

+ Keep clasped jars of chocolate-covered almonds or trail mix on the countertop, with a help-yourself policy. (Kids usually need help with portion control.) Don't fill the jar with your whole stash, which may disappear; hide half, and refill as needed.

+ Keep cookie dough in the refrigerator or freezer for quick baking.

+ Serve cheese. (It's filling.)

CHILAQUILES V. MIGAS

Do you ever wonder why tortillas come in giant stacks you can't use before they go dry and stale? Chilaquiles and migas is why: two genius techniques for using up stale (or going-stale) corn tortillas or tortilla chips, with eggs. You haven't lived until you've eaten a giant plate of these on a slow Saturday morning, with coffee and Tabasco sauce.

Chilaquiles are for the real tortilla lover: heavy on the fried tortillas, topped with fried egg, cheese, avocado, and pickled onions. Think of them like a breakfast nacho, but way more beautiful. Migas, on the other hand, are for the loaded-scrambled egg lover: eggs, lightly scrambled with peppers, tomatoes, and tortilla chips, which turn into a soft, swoony breakfast feast in the pan. Either can be a recklessly delicious weekend brunch that you've waited all week for, or a hero throw-together breakfast to use up the last tortillas in the bag.

HOW TO FRY TORTILLAS

Slice a small stack (about 4) of soft corn tortillas into thin strips or wedges. Warm about ½ inch (12 mm) canola oil in a large saucepan over medium-high heat. When it is sizzling hot (test it with a tiny droplet of water), add the tortillas and cook, turning once with tongs, until golden and brown. Transfer to a paper towel–lined plate and continue until all the chips are crispy brown.

HOW TO MAKE CHILAQUILES

In the same pan you used to fry the tortillas, spoon off the excess oil; add **a small can of crushed tomato plus 1 minced or pressed garlic clove, or your favorite jarred salsa**, and let it sizzle. Add the **tortilla chips** and cook, stirring to coat and soften the chips, for about 5 minutes. Serve them on a platter or individual plates topped with **fried eggs, cotija cheese, avocado, plain yogurt, pickled onions, fresh cilantro**, and **wedges of lime** on the side.

HOW TO MAKE MIGAS

Melt some **butter or oil** in a large skillet over medium-high heat. Add **1 small chopped onion, 1 finely chopped pepper** (hot or not; I like a red serrano), and **1 chopped bell pepper** (any color) and cook until soft and a little golden, 3 to 4 minutes. Add **1 chopped tomato** and the **crisped corn tortillas or chips**, stirring to coat. Lower the heat, then pour in **6 to 12 cracked and beaten eggs** (depending on how many you're feeding). Stir with a wooden spoon to make large, creamy curds. Remove from the heat and serve right in the skillet, or scoop onto individual plates and top with **cotija cheese, avocado, and fresh cilantro**.

TOAST
BREAD

ULTIMATE BACON, EGG, AND AVOCADO TOAST WITH TURMERIC DRIZZLE

TOTAL TIME: **10 MINUTES**

SERVES **4**

You don't need me to tell you how good bacon and eggs are together. Do take the nudge to add the turmeric drizzle, expressly for those who like to go beyond the ordinary.

LEMON-TURMERIC DRIZZLE

Juice of 1 lemon

¼ cup (60 ml) olive oil

¼ cup (60 ml) honey

1 tsp ground turmeric

Splash of cider vinegar

8 slices thick-cut bacon (preferably nitrate-free)

4 eggs

4 slices thick-cut sourdough bread

Butter or olive oil, for the bread

Crème fraîche (optional)

2 firm ripe avocados, sliced

Flaky sea salt, such as Maldon

Freshly ground black pepper

Tender greens or shoots, for garnish

TO MAKE THE LEMON-TURMERIC DRIZZLE: Stir together the lemon juice, oil, honey, turmeric, and vinegar, and set aside while you prepare the bacon and eggs.

Cook the bacon in a skillet until crispy and brown. Drain on a paper towel, and pour off a little fat from the skillet. Fry the eggs in the skillet until crispy and golden around the edges and the yolk is barely set, 4 to 5 minutes for runny (for a slightly firmer yolk, cover the pan in the last minute).

Meanwhile, toast the bread and brush evenly with butter.

Spread the crème fraîche (if using) on the toast, then layer the bacon, avocado, egg, and greens on top. Spoon over the lemon-turmeric drizzle. Serve warm.

MOROCCAN TOMATO TOAST

PREP TIME: **5 MINUTES**

TOTAL TIME: **20 MINUTES**

SERVES **4**

Something as simple as crushed coriander seeds and a hit of honey can bring an already good tomato to greatness. Spoon this mixture onto day-old toasted bread—thick or thin—over a bowl of plain yogurt, fish, a fried egg . . . you get the idea. It's better than salsa, in my opinion, but just as versatile.

1 cup (140 g) finely chopped red onion

½ tsp cumin seeds

¼ tsp fresh coriander seeds

4 slices thick-cut sourdough bread

Butter, for the bread

2 cups (280 g) chopped in-season tomatoes

3 Tbsp olive oil

¼ tsp flaky sea salt, such as Maldon

Fresh flowering or young herbs, such as cilantro, chopped

Light honey, such as wildflower, for drizzling

Soak the onion in a bowl of ice water to take out the bite, 5 to 10 minutes.

Toast the cumin and coriander in a dry skillet over high heat until fragrant, about 2 minutes. Smash slightly on a cutting board with the bottom of your (cooled) skillet, or with the back of your knife.

Toast the bread. Spread the toast with a thin schmear of butter or drizzle of oil.

Drain the onion well. Toss the cumin and coriander, onion, tomatoes, oil, and salt together in a bowl. Stir in the herbs. Spoon over the toast and drizzle very lightly with a bit of honey.

Get Ahead

These flavors get richer with time. Make the tomato mixture up to several hours ahead and let it sit, at room temperature, until ready to serve.

Golden Rule

I love yellow tomatoes for this because they are sweeter and less acidic than red, but any juicy tomatoes work.

Think of tahini toast as peanut butter toast's chic older sister. She's always got the latest fashion, all dolled up with her lemon juice and black sesame seeds. But, as I learned from my friend Lindsay Hunt (author of the cookbook *Healthyish*), she has a wild side, too, and never minds a dollop of tangy orange marmalade or chunky strawberry preserves on top. Of course, you need to start with a quality jar of tahini. If that's too hard to find, peanut or almond butter works with these toppings, too.

4 slices thick-cut bread

Butter or olive oil, for the bread

¼ cup (55 g) tahini

Honey or orange marmalade,
or any other preserves

Black sesame seeds

1 lemon, quartered

Toast the bread and brush evenly with butter. Spread the tahini on the toast and drizzle with honey or top with a healthy dollop of marmalade and sprinkle with sesame seeds. Squeeze with lemon and eat with gusto.

TAHINI TOAST WITH LEMON AND HONEY

TOTAL TIME: **5 MINUTES**

SERVES **4**

TAHINI

It's not hard to make your own tahini, if you can't find one you like. Toast 1 cup (140 g) hulled sesame seeds in a dry skillet until fragrant and lightly browned, 3 to 5 minutes. Let cool. Pulse in a food processor with 3 tablespoons canola or avocado oil and a pinch of salt until smooth. Store in the refrigerator for up to 1 month.

We stock bananas in the double digits. They're not quite one of our ten favorite foods, but an easy stalwart in a life with kids. The fallout, though, is bananas of varying ripeness in all parts of the house (or the smashed, *carried it all day in my purse* banana that gets stuck back in the fridge).

There are two solves: smoothies and banana bread. This lovely bread—as inviting as a breakfast bread as it is an afternoon snack—is a reinvention of the one my mom made nearly weekly back home. I've subbed in almond flour and oats for some of the white flour, and applesauce and maple syrup for the white sugar, but it's every bit as sweet and tender as hers. I alternate making this with nuts or with chocolate, but I'll let you guess which my family prefers.

NOT MY MAMA'S BANANA BREAD

PREP TIME: **15 MINUTES**

TOTAL TIME: 1½ **HOURS**

SERVES **8 TO 12**
(makes 2 loaves)

1 cup (220 g) coconut oil or (2 sticks) unsalted butter, at room temperature, plus more for the pan

1 cup (225 g) applesauce

¼ cup (60 ml) pure maple syrup

4 large eggs, at room temperature

2 tsp pure vanilla extract

2 cups (280 g) all-purpose flour or (310 g) gluten-free flour, plus more for the pan

1 cup (120 g) almond flour

1 cup (100 g) quick-cooking or rolled oats

2 tsp baking powder

1 tsp baking soda

1 tsp fine sea salt

2 cups (450 g) mashed bananas (about 4 very ripe bananas)

1 cup (about 120 g) chopped walnuts, pecans, and/or 70% dark chocolate

Preheat the oven to 350°F (180°C), with the racks in the middle third. Grease two 8½ by 4½ inch (21.5 by 11 cm) loaf pans and coat lightly with flour. Tap to release any excess flour.

cont'd

Beat the coconut oil in a large bowl until smooth. (If you're using butter, it will be creamy and light. The coconut oil will not be.) Add the applesauce and maple syrup and beat until mostly uniform. (If any of your ingredients are cold, the mixture will seem to curdle and separate; beat until uniform and smooth.) Add the eggs one at a time, along with the vanilla.

In a separate bowl, whisk together the flours, oats, baking powder, baking soda, and salt. Add the dry ingredients to the wet ingredients, alternating with the bananas, and mix until just combined. Fold in the nuts and/or chocolate.

Transfer the batter to the prepared pans and bake until it springs back lightly when touched, about 1 hour.

Serve warm, or let cool completely, wrap tightly in plastic wrap, and keep for up to 2 days in an airtight container.

GET AHEAD

This is a great bake-ahead because quick breads are almost always better when they sit overnight, uncut, totally cool, and well wrapped (bakers call it "ripening" their bread). Bake this a day or up to 2 days before serving. Because homemade breads have no preservatives, wrap well and freeze if you plan to keep it longer.

GOOD TO KNOW

If you, like me, often freeze overly ripe bananas and come back to them later, you know that they lose moisture content, and a fragrant banana liquor seeps out as they defrost. This can yield a tiny banana with tons of liquor, and you could pack almost 4 of these droopy bananas into 1 cup (225 g). Don't be tempted to use more bananas for this recipe; instead, use the 4 bananas suggested, and all the banana liquor to equal 2 cups (450 g). This should yield just the right amount of flavor and liquid to make the texture a dream.

By two o'clock most days, all I can think about is chocolate. If you're a chocolate person, you get this: Sometimes a sliver of bittersweet will do, but sometimes you need something a little more toothsome, like cake, but not quite—something *really* satisfying to tide you over until dinner with a big smile.

This is that sort of thing: perfect for after school, tea with a friend, or even a late-morning snack on a special kind of day (read: big test, big meeting, big birthday kind of day). It's delicious on the spot, but the fudgy qualities deepen each day, giving you a two o'clock chocolate fix for the whole week.

10 oz (280 g) semisweet chocolate, chopped

2 cups (480 ml) buttermilk

2 cups (280 g) all-purpose or (310 g) gluten-free flour, plus more for the pan

¾ cup (60 g) Dutch-process cocoa powder, plus more for the pan

1¼ tsp baking powder

¼ tsp baking soda

1½ cups (3 sticks) unsalted butter

1 cup (200 g) unbleached granulated sugar

1 cup (200 g) coconut sugar or dark brown sugar

5 large eggs

Preheat the oven to 325°F (165°C) with the rack in the middle. Butter two 8½ by 4½ inch (21.5 by 11 cm) loaf pans and coat lightly with a mixture of cocoa and flour. Tap to release any excess cocoa and flour.

Place 6 ounces (170 g) of the chocolate (a little more than half) in a heatproof bowl. Bring the buttermilk to a simmer in a saucepan over medium heat. Pour over the chocolate in the bowl and set aside until melted; whisk together until smooth and let cool to room temperature.

cont'd

CHOCOLATE SNACKING LOAF

PREP TIME: **30 MINUTES**

TOTAL TIME: **1 HOUR 10 MINUTES**

SERVES **8 TO 12**
(makes 2 loaves)

Meanwhile, whisk together the flour, cocoa powder, baking powder, and baking soda in a bowl. Beat the butter and sugars together in an electric mixer fitted with the paddle attachment on medium speed until light and fluffy, about 5 minutes, scraping down the bowl halfway through. Add the eggs one at a time, mixing well after each one (the eggs may look slightly curdled—don't worry, keep beating). Add the flour mixture one-third at a time, alternating with the chocolate mixture, and stir gently until completely combined. Stir in the remaining 4 ounces (110 g) chopped chocolate.

Transfer to the prepared pans and bake the loaves on the middle rack until a toothpick inserted in the center comes out with just a few crumbs, about 1 hour. Be careful not to overbake; you want the inside to still be moist. Let cool completely on a rack before unmolding.

GET AHEAD
This loaf is a perfect make-ahead snack because it is best on day two, when all the fudgy goodness comes to life. Bake this a day or up to 2 days before serving. Because homemade breads have no preservatives, wrap well and freeze if you plan to keep it longer.

GOOD TO KNOW
If it's a fancier cake you crave, bake all of the batter in a single Bundt pan at the same temperature for about 1 hour 30 minutes.

When I moved to New York City fresh from college, I had a boyfriend who'd spent a year living in Majorca, Spain. Every morning for breakfast, he ate toast with smashed avocado, a squeeze of lemon, and salt—a habit he'd picked up on the island. A decade later, when avo toast was mega-trending, my parents traveled to Spain and told me about the most incredible thing they ate during their stay: toasted bread lavished with oil, smashed avocado, lemon, and salt.

It makes no difference when you first discovered avocado toast: two decades or two days ago. It's delicious. But it's the creamy and unctuous avocado doing the heavy lifting, so don't save them just for toast. Here are my favorite ways to eat one (with or without toast), without ever tiring of its virtues:

ODE TO AVOCADO

+ Serve on rice with bacon and fried eggs. (Bonus: Add steamed greens or sliced radish.)

+ Smash on toast and top with purple radish, green sauce (page 220), and a fried egg.

+ Serve chopped on cooked red lentils (dal) with yogurt and scallion.

+ Puree into classic hummus with extra lemon or lime (to preserve color).

+ Chop and add to a baked potato with Easy Smoky Black Beans (page 148) and sour cream.

+ Tuck into whole-grain bread with cucumber, spinach, and yogurt or tzatziki.

+ Toss with cubed cucumber, watermelon, and feta; drizzle with oil and lemon juice; and sprinkle with flaky salt.

+ Toss with shredded cooked chicken (page 126), halved cherry tomatoes, hard-boiled eggs, romaine, and bacon for a deluxe Cobb salad.

+ Layer with poached salmon (page 228), Dijon, and lettuce on a soft roll.

+ Serve on toast with poached eggs and Tahini Green Goddess Dressing (page 223).

I don't love making salad—washing, chopping, and fussing over greens and vegetables—but I *love* eating salad. One summer, trying to feed us all well between a glut of parties and fairs, I fell back on my old standby: Greek salad. I started with the classic—hunks of cucumbers, onion, feta, and olives, but as I subbed in any other vegetables that appeared in my CSA box week by week—fennel, peaches, tomatillos—it hit me: Greek salad isn't just a salad, it's a formula, and the best one for winning at getting more vegetables on your plate.

Try it! It goes like this: big meaty chunks of vegetables + large amounts of a salty, flavorful cheese (cut or crumbled) + olives (or capers) + dressing (anything you have stashed in the refrigerator, or a drizzle of olive oil, lemon, and salt and pepper if you don't). The result: big smiles, full bellies.

GREEK SALAD (SORT OF)

TOTAL TIME: **10 MINUTES**

SERVES **4**

1 cucumber or zucchini, peeled or unpeeled, coarsely chopped

1 pepper (any kind, hot or sweet), seeded and chopped

1 tomato, tomatillo, peach, or plum (something juicy and slightly sweet and tangy), chopped

1 handful of washed greens or other leaves

1 small red or white onion, chopped (optional)

6 oz (170 g) salty semifirm cheese like feta or aged goat cheese

½ cup (70 g) olives, pitted

1 small handful of fresh tender herbs (like dill or chives)

Olive oil and lemon juice, for drizzling

Flaky sea salt, such as Maldon

Freshly ground black pepper

Toss all the ingredients together in a large bowl, seasoning to taste with salt and pepper. Set aside for the salt and pepper to draw out flavor and lightly soften the vegetables, about 5 minutes, before serving.

RADISH SALAD WITH KALE, ALMONDS, AND PARM

PREP TIME: **5 MINUTES**

TOTAL TIME: **10 MINUTES**

SERVES **4**

This cold-season, trick-up-your-sleeve salad goes with almost any meal. It's killer with charcuterie as a simple lunch, but don't stop there. It's a beauty to plate up for guests, on individual plates or one large platter. And, because kale takes some time to break down and become tender, making it ahead isn't only possible, it's the best way to go.

½ head Tuscan kale, cut or torn into bite-size pieces

3 Tbsp high-quality extra-virgin olive oil

Juice of ½ lemon

Fine sea salt

Freshly ground black pepper

1 large black, purple, or watermelon radish, thinly sliced or cut into bite-size pieces

2 small Tokyo turnips or small radishes, thinly sliced

4 oz (115 g) Parmesan cheese, broken into bits

⅓ cup (40 g) roasted unsalted almonds, coarsely chopped

Flaky sea salt, such as Maldon, for serving

Toss the kale together with the oil and lemon juice in a large bowl. Season with fine salt and pepper. Massage the kale, squeezing and rubbing the leaves together with your hands, working the oil, lemon juice, salt, and pepper into the leaves to flavor and tenderize them. Toss together with the radish, turnips, cheese, and almonds. Divide among serving plates and garnish with flaky salt and more pepper. Serve at room temperature.

GET AHEAD

Kale tenderizes as it sits in lemon and salt, so making this a day ahead always works. Keep in an airtight container in the refrigerator for up to 2 days. Radishes, too, can benefit from some softening, but after a day they get stinky, so if you're planning to keep the salad for more than half a day, throw your radishes in no more than a few hours before serving.

This meal in a bowl, heaped with good-for-you ingredients and potent flavor to boot, is my midday stalwart. This is, ideally, a lunch to throw together with the bits and bubs in the leftovers from other main events: Let's say you grilled or roasted vegetables on the weekend, and have some (any, really) leftover grains lying around. Great, today's lunch will be easy.

If you *don't* have leftover veggies or grains, I've given you the instructions for those on the spot. Sock away extras for easy lunches for the rest of the week.

GREEN GODDESS SALAD BOWLS

PREP TIME: **15 MINUTES**
TOTAL TIME: **35 MINUTES**
SERVES **4**

1½ cups (300 g) uncooked red or brown rice

½ cup (90 g) uncooked red or white quinoa

1 large eggplant (about 2 lb/910 g), cut into 2-inch (5-cm) pieces

2 large zucchini (about 2 lb/910 g total), cut into 2-inch (5-cm) pieces

2 red onions, cut into eighths

⅓ cup (80 ml) extra-virgin olive oil

½ tsp za'atar or ground coriander

1 tsp flaky sea salt, such as Maldon

3 cups (45 g) baby kale or spinach

Tahini Green Goddess Dressing (page 223)

½ cup (60 g) toasted almonds, coarsely chopped

Any dry, semisoft cheese, such as ricotta salata or cotija, for serving

Cook the rice and quinoa together in 4 cups (1 L) water, in a rice cooker, or on the stovetop until just tender.

Meanwhile, heat a grill or grill pan to medium-high. Toss the eggplant, zucchini, and onions with the oil, za'atar, and salt. Grill, turning once, until tender and nicely charred, 4 to 6 minutes per side. Set aside to cool slightly.

Toss the vegetables, kale, and about ½ cup (120 ml) of the dressing together in a large bowl. Spoon the warm rice and quinoa into bowls. Scoop the dressed vegetables over the grains. Serve warm, topped with almonds and cheese, with extra dressing on the side.

GET AHEAD

Use a rice cooker or Instant Pot to simplify your prep and keep cooked grains at the ready—you need 3 to 4 cups (360 to 480 g) cooked grains for four heaping goddess bowls. Grill or roast (see Roasting Day!, page 236) vegetables and store in airtight containers in the refrigerator for up to 4 days. Reheat in a shallow pan with just a splash of olive oil, over low heat. Almonds can be chopped and kept in zipped bags or airtight containers at room temperature for up to 1 week or in the refrigerator for 2 weeks.

THINK FAST

If your grain bank is empty, and you don't have time to cook fresh ones, serve everything on a bed of warm couscous, which cooks in 5 minutes.

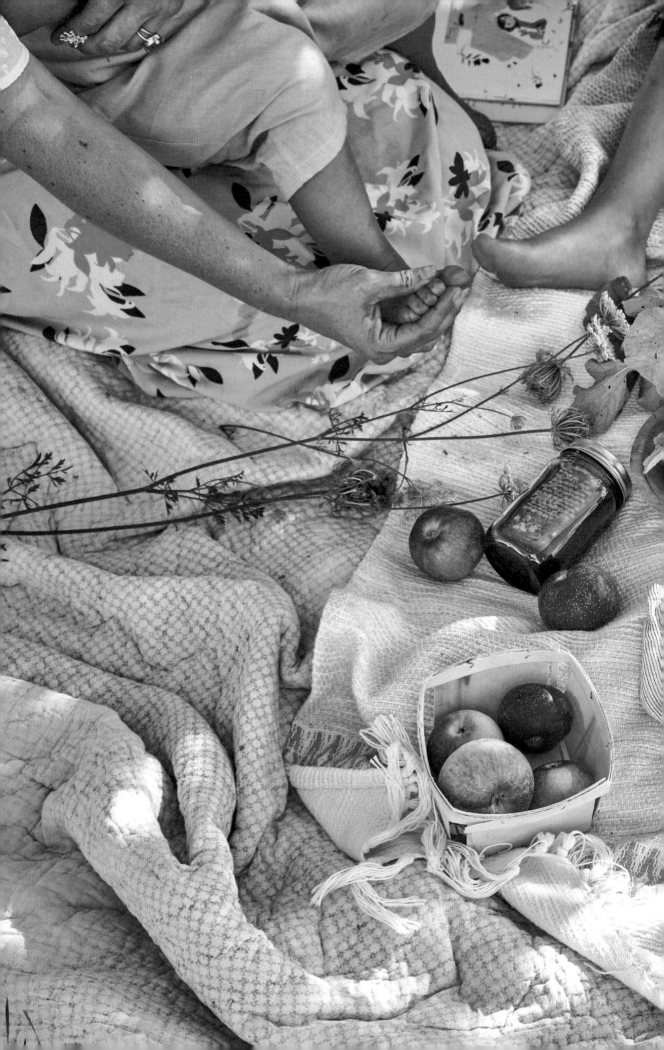

My family calls this magic soup, because there's always a pot on and it never seems to run out. This is the thing to make when you've gotten too ambitious at the farmers' market or grocery store, or when you need to finish the dregs of the vegetable drawer before the next lot comes in—it turns a hodgepodge of loose vegetables into a meal in no time.

Don't be afraid to improvise. The key here is a flavorful broth, and a little fat (butter or oil) to round out this satisfying soup. I almost always put a bit of squash or sweet potato in my vegetable soup, especially if I don't have a particularly rich broth lying around. It adds a subtle soft sweetness to the mix; therein lies the *real* magic.

ALWAYS-ON VEGETABLE SOUP

PREP TIME: **25 MINUTES**

TOTAL TIME: **1 HOUR**

SERVES **4 TO 6**

2 Tbsp olive oil, plus more for serving

½ onion, chopped

2 to 3 garlic cloves, smashed or roughly chopped

1 stalk celery, chopped

2 carrots, chopped or sliced

Fine sea salt

Freshly ground black pepper

8 cups (2 L) chicken or vegetable broth (page 126 or 225)

One 14-oz (400-g) can tomatoes or a handful of chopped fresh tomatoes

1 bay leaf

1 piece of Parmesan rind (any size), plus grated Parmesan cheese for serving

2 heaping cups (about 250 g) mixed vegetables (squash, zucchini, sweet potato, white potato, green beans), cut into bite-size pieces

One 15.5-oz (439-g) can beans (such as cannellini, chickpeas, or navy beans), rinsed and drained (optional)

2 Tbsp unsalted butter (optional)

Heat the oil in a large pot over medium heat. Add the onion, garlic, celery, carrots, and a bit of salt and pepper. Cook, stirring from time to time, until the onion is translucent, 5 to 8 minutes.

Add the broth, the tomatoes, and their juice—squeezing the tomatoes through your fingers—to the pot, along with the bay leaf and Parmesan rind. Bring the soup to a boil, lower the heat, and simmer, uncovered, for 20 minutes. Add the remaining vegetables and the beans, if using, to the pot and continue to cook until all the vegetables are tender, about 20 minutes more. Stir in the butter to add richness (if desired) and season with salt.

Remove the Parmesan rind and bay leaf, and ladle the soup into bowls. Sprinkle with grated Parmesan, drizzle with additional oil, if desired, and serve.

GET AHEAD
This soup holds like a dream. Make, cool, and store in an airtight container in the refrigerator for up to 3 days, or the freezer for up to 3 weeks. I never add greens or beans when I'm making it ahead, but stir them in during the reheat.

GOOD TO KNOW
This is a great lazy chef's soup. I often use a smashed clove of garlic, because I don't believe in fussy cooking and don't like strong garlic flavors in an otherwise balanced soup. Remove it before eating, if you like, though the whole clove softens during cooking, and can be eaten by the lucky person whose bowl it lands in. If you use young or delicate squash (such as delicata, or a small butternut or honey nut), there's no need to peel your squash before adding—the edible skin softens while cooking.

MORE MAGIC SOUP
When there's, say, a cup or so of soup left in the pot, but not enough for another meal, add more veggies, a bit of water, and maybe another can of beans and tomorrow you can feed the family again. Just before serving, add a handful or two of finely chopped or thinly sliced spinach, kale, collards, Swiss chard, or even parsley for a bright finish and extra vitamin C. Sprinkle grated Parm over the top.

CREAMY MUSHROOM SOUP

PREP TIME: **30 MINUTES**

TOTAL TIME: **1½ HOURS**

SERVES **6 TO 8**
(makes 9 cups/2.1 L)

The best mushroom soups I've ever had were in Hungary, where my husband is from. There, we eat them year-round, but especially in fall and spring, when the rains are coming down and the mushrooms are popping up. A good one should be chock-full of mushrooms, the most interesting ones you can find. You'll need to take your time coaxing out their flavor, so plan on making this ahead; it only gets better with time.

Also: There are beans in this soup. Don't worry, you won't taste them. I didn't learn to love beans until I married a vegetarian and discovered beans' secret powers for turning ordinary mushroom soup into a rich cream-of-mushroom soup. Round this one out with a good bread and a hearty salad, if you're a big meal kind of crew. We're a double bowl of soup crew over here, and this soup goes quick.

2 Tbsp olive oil

6 Tbsp (¾ stick) unsalted butter

2 small yellow onions, finely chopped (about 3 cups/420 g)

8 garlic cloves, smashed

2 sprigs fresh thyme

One 15-oz (425-g) can cannellini beans, rinsed and drained

One 1-oz (30-g) package dried mushrooms, such as porcini or shiitake

4 cups (960 ml) boiling water

1½ lb (about 10 cups/600 g) mixed fresh wild mushrooms, such as oyster or cremini

2 tsp fine sea salt

Freshly ground black pepper

2 tsp soy sauce or tamari

¼ cup (8 g) finely grated Parmesan cheese

½ to 1 cup (120 to 240 ml) heavy cream

Chopped fresh dill, for serving (optional)

1 baguette, for serving (see Garlic Bread, facing page)

Heat the oil and 2 tablespoons of the butter in a large saucepan over medium heat. Add the onions and garlic, and cook, stirring occasionally, until softened, about 5 minutes. Add the thyme and dried mushrooms, then pour in the boiling water. Return to a boil, then simmer over medium heat until the mushrooms plump, about 5 minutes. Cover and set aside for 15 minutes.

Meanwhile, melt an additional pat of butter in your largest skillet over high heat. Add the fresh mushrooms, a bit at a time, and cook until golden and soft, about 5 minutes, scooching cooked mushrooms off to a plate to make room for more as needed. Be patient here— the more crispy and golden the mushrooms get, the more flavorful the finished soup. Repeat with more butter and mushrooms, reserving 2 tablespoons butter for the end. Season the cooked mushrooms with up to 2 teaspoons salt (they need it, so don't be timid). Set aside.

Add the beans to the dried-mushroom broth and puree with an immersion blender until completely smooth. Stir in the cooked mushrooms, and process until there are some smooth mushrooms, but still plenty of meaty mushroom bites throughout; it's up to you how chunky or smooth you want the finished soup to be. Stir in the remaining 2 tablespoons butter and season as needed with tons of freshly cracked black pepper, soy sauce, and cheese (these flavors will intensify as the soup sits).

Stir in the cream and warm through, or, if you want a leaner soup, ladle into bowls and drizzle each serving lightly with cream. Sprinkle with dill, if desired, and serve warm with the bread.

GET AHEAD
This soup improves in flavor overnight, or even after an hour or two on the stove, so I almost always make it in advance. Because buying, cleaning, and chopping mushrooms can feel like a chore, I've given you a big-batch recipe, enough for a batch to serve and a second batch to freeze; halve this if that seems like too much work. Keep extras in the refrigerator for up to a week and the freezer for up to 1 month.

GOOD TO KNOW
Many people soak and then rinse their dried mushrooms before using to ensure there's no dirt. That's a little fussy for me, but if your dried mushrooms seem gritty, go for it. Also, if you want to get fancy, add a splash of brandy or cognac to the last batch of mushrooms for boosted flavor, the French way. When I don't have any (often), I use soy and Parmesan or both— especially if I'm using plain button mushrooms—to get the most oomph in every bite.

GARLIC BREAD
To make a quick garlic bread, add a baguette to your shopping list. Cut the baguette in half lengthwise, then into fourths (to make 8 long pieces). Brush the cut sides generously with olive oil, and toast under the broiler, on low, until just toasty brown. Remove from the broiler and rub the toast with a whole garlic clove.

POZOLE VERDE WITH AVOCADO AND RADISHES

PREP TIME: **20 MINUTES**

TOTAL TIME: **1 HOUR**

SERVES **6 TO 8**
(makes 10 cups/2.4 L)

Many cultures have given us wonderful soups, but the one I can't get enough of is pozole (or posole), a traditional Mexican soup that trumps all others for me.

There are a few types of pozole, but the one I like best is pozole verde (green pozole) with chicken, topped with radish, avocado, and cotija cheese. This method piggybacks on the poached chicken (page 126), so head there first. Whenever I poach a chicken, it is almost always with this soup in mind.

I'm not going to lie—this dirties a few dishes, and that's why I always make it ahead, but it's worth the effort. As for the toppings, which are a must, give yourself a head start there, too: clean and chop all but the avocado a day ahead, so you can throw a bowl of this ultra-satisfying soup on the table in the middle of any old day.

½ cup (70 g) pumpkin seeds

1 lb (455 g) tomatillos, husks removed

1 white onion, roughly chopped

3 poblano peppers, stems and seeds removed, coarsely chopped

6 cups (1.4 L) chicken broth (page 126)

1 tsp fine sea salt

1 handful of fresh cilantro leaves and fine stems

1 lb (455 g) poached chicken (from ½ chicken; page 126)

1 Tbsp extra-virgin olive oil

One 28-oz (800-g) can white hominy, drained (see Hominy, page 84)

TOPPINGS

1 firm, ripe avocado, chopped

4 radishes, sliced

1 fresh green chile, sliced

Fresh cilantro leaves, chopped

½ white onion, finely chopped (optional)

Cotija or queso fresco

cont'd

Heat the pumpkin seeds in a large Dutch oven over medium-high heat, stirring constantly, until they start to pop and smell nutty, about 4 minutes. Add the tomatillos, onion, peppers, broth, and the salt. Bring to a boil, then lower the heat and simmer, stirring occasionally, until the vegetables are completely tender, about 20 minutes. Pour into a strainer set over a bowl, reserving the broth. Puree the cooked vegetables in a blender, adding the cilantro (stems and leaves).

Meanwhile, shred the chicken into large chunks (you should have about 3½ cups/455 g) and set aside.

Add the oil to the Dutch oven and heat over high heat. Add the pureed vegetables and stir constantly or cover (to keep it from splattering) for about 15 seconds. Return the reserved broth to the pot, whisking it into the puree, and bring to a simmer. Stir in the chicken and hominy and cook until just warmed through. Spoon the soup into bowls and garnish with avocado, radishes, chile, cilantro, onion (if using), and cheese, and serve warm.

GET AHEAD
This soup holds well, and even keeps its gorgeous color for a day or two. Make, let cool, and store in an airtight container in the refrigerator for up to 3 days or the freezer for up to 3 weeks. Always add your toppings just before serving.

HOMINY
Hominy is a large white corn, dried and treated with lye or lime to soften the hulls, usually canned or frozen, that stars in this soup. Either keeps well for months, so I always buy it when I see it to have at the ready for this meal in a bowl.

This classic chowder is comforting and delicious on its own, but for a soup you won't soon forget, add a spoonful of the Basil-Poblano-Garlic Relish. I spoon this number on any soup, just like I use my favorite green sauce on any fish, chicken, or steak.

When corn season is over, make this chowder with potatoes alone (be sure to use chicken broth to boost flavor). I bet you'll love this version, too. Last little thing: This is *especially* good with heaps of freshly grated Parmesan over the top—and I mean heaps. Stir it in to both thicken the soup and amplify the flavor. Other tasty garnishes include scallions, chopped heirloom tomatoes, and more bacon, of course.

POTATO-CORN CHOWDER WITH BASIL-POBLANO-GARLIC RELISH

PREP TIME: **25 MINUTES**

TOTAL TIME: **40 MINUTES**

SERVES **6**
(makes 8 cups/2 L)

POTATO-CORN CHOWDER

1 to 2 slices bacon (depending on how much you like bacon), finely chopped

1 large yellow onion, finely chopped

3 to 4 ears of fresh corn (depending on how much you like corn)

1 tsp fine sea salt, plus more to taste

6 cups (1.4 L) chicken broth (page 126) or water

1 lb (455 g) small potatoes, quartered or halved (about 3 cups)

BASIL-POBLANO-GARLIC RELISH

2 large poblano peppers, seeds removed, finely chopped

¼ red onion, finely chopped

2 garlic cloves, minced or pressed

1 cup (40 g) fresh basil leaves, finely chopped (or baby leaves)

1 Tbsp olive oil

TO FINISH

Freshly ground black pepper

1 cup (240 ml) half-and-half or milk

Finely grated Parmesan cheese

cont'd

TO MAKE THE POTATO-CORN CHOWDER: Cook the bacon in a large pot over medium heat until brown and just starting to get crispy, about 6 minutes. Add the yellow onion and cook, stirring, until soft and golden, 4 to 6 minutes.

Meanwhile, cut the corn kernels from the ears with a sharp knife and reserve the cobs. Add the corn kernels, salt, and broth to the pot with the bacon. Use the back of the knife to scrape and "milk" the corn cobs, scraping all the leftover kernels and milky white liquid into the pot; add the cobs to the pot, along with the potatoes. Bring to a simmer and cook for about 20 minutes.

WHILE THE SOUP SIMMERS, MAKE THE BASIL-POBLANO-GARLIC RELISH: In a small bowl, combine the poblano peppers, red onion, garlic, and basil, and toss gently with a spoon. Just before serving, add the oil and toss to make a loose relish.

Taste your broth and add salt or black pepper as needed. When it's seasoned to your liking, remove the corn cobs and discard. Add the half-and-half a bit at a time, stopping when it reaches a consistency you love. (Some like their soup creamy, some chunky, some brothy—you be the judge.) Mash about half the potatoes and corn with a potato masher, and keep warm over low heat.

Ladle the soup into bowls and spoon the relish and any oil over the top. Top with cheese.

GET AHEAD

Like so many good soups, this gets better on the second day. The flavors intensify, and I love the way the soup thickens when reheated on day two (thanks to the potatoes breaking down). Store in the refrigerator for up to 2 days, or freeze for 1 week. You can also chop the poblanos, red onion, and garlic and keep the mixture in the refrigerator, sans basil, for up to 4 days.

POBLANO GRILLED CHEESE

Once you get hooked on the poblano-onion-garlic-basil goodness, you may be looking for other places to relive this flavor combo. Since this recipe makes 3 cups (420 g) of relish, I've been known to sprinkle leftovers on thinly sliced mozzarella between two slices of buttered whole-grain bread and press the whole lot into a punchy grilled cheese.

This classic combination is akin to the infamous sal-ade Niçoise of France with a bit of Italian influence. Repeat this satisfying dish from spring to fall (though spring is high season for the main ingredients); it's as easy to prepare as it is gorgeous. This is one of those sum-of-its-parts stories: simple ingredients that, together, shine.

8 oz (226 g) small potatoes, such as fingerlings or new potatoes

2 Tbsp red wine vinegar or sherry vinegar

6 Tbsp extra-virgin olive oil

Fine sea salt

Freshly ground black pepper

1 handful (about 4 oz/115 g) of green, yellow, or purple wax beans, trimmed

¼ small red onion, thinly sliced

¼ cup (35 g) plump green olives, such as Castelvetranos, pitted

1 Tbsp capers, plus brine

¼ cup (10 g) fresh flat-leaf parsley leaves or tarragon, or both

4 anchovy fillets (optional)

4 hard-boiled eggs, peeled and cut into quarters

Flaky sea salt, such as Maldon

Put the potatoes in a pot, cover with heavily salted water, and bring to a boil. Cook until tender, about 20 to 25 minutes. Drain, reserving a little of the cooking liquid.

Meanwhile, whisk together the vinegar, oil, 1 teaspoon fine salt, and pepper to taste, and set aside.

Cut the cooked potatoes into quarters (if large) or halves (if small) and arrange them on a platter in an even layer. Spoon over about ⅓ cup (80 ml) of the dressing and set aside while you prepare the rest of the salad.

cont'd

YELLOW BEAN SALAD WITH POTATOES, CAPERS, AND EGGS

PREP TIME: **15 MINUTES**

TOTAL TIME: **30 MINUTES**

SERVES **4**

Bring another pot of water to a boil, with a bowl of salted ice water ready nearby. Drop the green beans into the boiling water; when their color is deeply saturated (a couple of minutes), transfer them to the ice water to stop the cooking. Drain and pat them dry.

Toss the beans, onion, olives, capers (with their brine), parsley, and anchovies (if using) together with the remaining dressing in a large bowl, then transfer to the platter. Add the eggs, sprinkle with flaky salt, and serve at room temperature.

GET AHEAD

Cook your potatoes and blanch your green beans; drain, cover tightly, and refrigerate until ready to use, up to 2 days for the beans and 4 days for the potatoes. Bring to room temperature before cutting the potatoes and assembling the salad.

MAKE YOUR YOGURT WORK FOR YOU

Most of the recipes in this chapter come with flavor built in. But sometimes you need a midday meal that doesn't take any thought, one that works well with the things in your refrigerator. If yogurt is in there, you can quickly turn it into one of these four easy dips, a unifying force to dollop or spread on an otherwise lackluster sandwich or, my go-to, plain ol' fried eggs and fresh greens, and make something worth repeating. Each makes about 1 heaping cup (240 g), and keeps well in an airtight container in the refrigerator for up to 3 days.

QUICKIE TZATZIKI: Grate ½ small or hothouse cucumber on a box grater. Stir into 1 cup (240 g) plain Greek or full-fat yogurt with 1 pressed or minced garlic clove, 2 tablespoons chopped fresh dill, ¼ teaspoon fine sea salt, and ¼ teaspoon freshly ground black pepper. Stir in grated lemon zest and lemon juice to taste (about ½ teaspoon zest and 1 teaspoon juice). Great with: hummus, toasted pita, roasted vegetables.

BROWN BUTTER HERB DIP: Cook ¼ cup (½ stick) unsalted butter in a pan over low heat until toasty and brown. Chop any herbs in the refrigerator to make ¼ cup (20 g). Gently fold the herbs, brown butter, and ¼ teaspoon fine sea salt into 1 cup (240 g) plain Greek or full-fat yogurt. Great with: fish, sliced tomatoes, roasted vegetables, cooked beets.

CHILE-LEMON SAUCE: Stir the grated zest and juice of 1 lemon, a scant ¼ cup (10 g) finely chopped fresh parsley, 1 pressed or minced garlic clove, and 1 tablespoon hot pepper paste into 1 cup (240 g) plain Greek or full-fat yogurt. Great with: chicken, roasted potatoes, fried eggs.

HORSERADISH CREAM: Stir 1 to 2 tablespoons (depending on your taste) grated (prepared) horseradish, the grated zest of ½ lemon, 3 tablespoons finely chopped fresh chives, and ¼ teaspoon fine sea salt into 1 cup (240 g) plain Greek or full-fat yogurt. Great with: roast beef, beets, leftover short-rib sandwiches.

GRAZIN
PLATTE

HUNGARIAN SNACKING TRAY

In Hungary, where we travel each summer, almost every stop in to friends or family centers around epic meat and cheese boards featuring everything under the sun: sausages, Trappist cheeses, and loads of wax peppers, snappy cucumbers, and spring onions plucked straight from the soil. There's plenty of buttered bread to pile it all on, plus eggs, mustard, sauerkraut, and pickles—dozens of pickles. The idea: Your guests can eat as little (or more likely as much) as they want, and leave the rest, with zero formality. This jives with me rather well.

A proper snack tray in Hungary is teeming with sweets—doughy and poppy seed laced, or crumbly and tart. There might be butter cookies in a tin or savory cheese biscuits wrapped in a linen, and flaky stuffed strudels that disappear in a breath. No matter how unaccomplished at baking your hosts consider themselves, there will always be something deliciously home baked and there will be zero rules about eating your vegetables first. This jives with my children rather well.

It doesn't matter if you've never been to Hungary, or never will; you can adopt this way of life as your own. Here's how to make like a Hungarian and really live a little.

MEAT: If you can find it, goose liver pâté is a hallmark of Hungarian cuisine, but any pâté—like Easy Chicken Liver Pâté (page 218)—works great, or even liverwurst if that's what you can find. Add ham, and plenty of sausages, thinly sliced; both *csipos* (hot) and *édes* (sweet) are welcome, though any dried Hungarian, French, or Italian sausage will do the trick.

CHEESE: Semisoft Trappist monk cheeses go splendidly with this spread, but there is plenty of room for interpretation. A round of soft and funky tomme, or a wedge of harder German or Alpine cheese would be right at home here. Consider your crowd and work from there.

PEPPERS: You can hunt down pale green and slightly spicy Hungarian wax peppers, as they are distinct and delicious on top of buttered bread. In their stead, use banana peppers. They're milder, but have the same crisp edge.

OTHER VEGETABLES: Radishes, cucumbers, and fresh spring onions or scallions, sliced thinly or served whole (with a knife handy for DIY slicing), are a must for layering with cheese and meat into open-faced sandwiches.

EGGS: Hard-boiled or pickled eggs are great pick-up-and-eat foods and beautiful in the mix.

BREAD: White bread, brown bread, rye bread, cheese biscuits—anything works here.

BUTTER: European-style or cultured, lightly salted butter is a treat, or use a fresh local butter (a small splurge, but think of it like cheese). Butter the bread in advance or let guests DIY.

MUSTARD: A single pot of strong mustard, like smooth or grainy Dijon, goes a long way.

FRUIT: Anything perfectly ripe and in season belongs. In Hungary, wine grapes, small apples, plums, sweet cherries, figs, pears, and apricots are usually included, depending on the season. Add your favorites, fresh or dried.

SWEETS: They're a must. Our favorites: poppy, apple, or sour-cherry strudel; walnut beigli; Russian tea cakes; or any other nutty, fruity, not-too-sweet pastry.

THE BEST WHITE-BREAD SANDWICHES

When I was a kid, family parties happened three times a year: New Year's Eve, the Fourth of July, and graduation. If you were from a big family in a neighborhood of big families, you might be on the graduation circuit for a decade.

The go-to fare to serve a crowd in this era was giant sub sandwiches that ran the length of a long folding table (plastic or polyester cloth–covered, always). The sandwich, cut in towering meat-and-cheese-packed hunks, was always on white bread. If memory serves, it more than did the job. But there's an easier feed-a-crowd sandwich, which has the added benefit of being vegetarian and vegan friendly, and beautifully chic, too. Take inspiration from the humble but genius tomato sandwich (you know: white bread, mayo, perfectly ripe juicy tomatoes), but make a show of it. Offer all the possible breads, fixings, toppings, and spreads, gorgeously arranged on platters and trays for your crowd to stack and slice their own sandwiches as they see fit.

BREAD: Lay out towering stacks on a platter; it can be thin sliced white bread, or thick slices of ciabatta or sourdough, or sliced seeded whole-grain or a gluten-free option, depending on your crowd.

MAYO: Straight up and classic, please. Be generous. It seals the bread and keeps it from getting soggy from the next ingredient on the list. Decant into a bowl or go low-brow chic with a jar and a classy knife.

TOMATOES: Heirloom tomatoes, fresh from a farm or a garden, are a deserving star of this spread. Slice them thick, salt them, and let them drain on paper towels for an hour; transfer to a platter to serve.

CUCUMBERS: Small, fresh, snappy cucumbers add a crunchy edge and color (whether your guests put them in their sandwiches or eat them on their own).

HERBS: Any fresh herbs are welcome here—dill, mint, parsley, oregano—but anything flowering, like chives, gets top marks. Stand sprigs and bunches in cups in water, like flowers, for guests to pick off, or finely chop them and serve in small bowls for sprinkling.

SALT: A potent sea salt, like Maldon or *fleur de sel*, is a win; leave it at the ready in copious amounts. It is the secret to extracting even more umami from every bite.

PEPPER: Freshly ground and generous is the key here. Include a pepper mill for self-service.

THE EVERYTHING LOX LUNCH

If I learned one thing in fifteen years as a New Yorker, it's that bagels and lox are always the answer to a crowd descending on your tiny space. I am an everything *on* my bagel kind of girl: crème fraîche, lox, red onions, capers, chives—give me all the toppings. For company, or even your own family, put out a platter of the freshest bagels you can get (smaller, not larger, are usually better). Then be lavish with topping options.

BAGELS: Plan on one bagel per person. Include a variety; sesame and poppy seed seem to always go first, so buy extra. Skip the blueberry.

SOMETHING CREAMY: Cream cheese is great, and crème fraîche is even better—it's easier to spread one-handed. Opt for plain, and let the toppings shine.

SMOKED FISH: Cured lox or gravlax should be moist looking, and beautifully sliced, with plump flesh. Hot-smoked salmon and any other smoked fish you can get your hands on belong, too. We love ultra-smoky trout and tender smoked whitefish with its shimmery golden skin. Lay them on a platter with a small fork for self-service.

TOMATOES: Even pale, off-season tomatoes work in this spread, but if you can, opt for small heirlooms (less juicy than their meatier counterparts) or medium-size brown tomatoes like Kumato. Slice them thin, and salt them.

ONIONS: Even if *you* don't love them yourself, onions are a must. Go for thinly sliced red onions, raw or pickled.

CAPERS: The ultimate lox garnish, capers and caper berries add signature tang. Tiny capers or sliced caper berries can be slipped under layers of lox to stay put.

DILL: Any fresh herbs make this spread more gorgeous, but dill will shine for its delicate flavor.

A GOURMAND'S WORKING LUNCH

As anyone who's worked with me knows, I consider a quiet sit-down lunch (without screens) the holy grail. This is sacred time. If you have a partner, roommates, or kids who think it's okay to reach onto your plate and help themselves at other meals, you know what I'm talking about.

This meal is the great reward for all the small investments you've made all week—the best way not to waste an ounce of your hard work. If you've already been working the plan in this book (stocking and stashing your favorite ingredients, simple sauces, and such), you'll have plenty of options to pull this off.

Yes, per the title, you can work during this lunch—just make sure it's, like, breathwork, or some other important task that feeds your soul.

GREENS: Make good on the last handful of any green leaves in the refrigerator or the leavings of last night's salad, like a hearty kale number that doesn't wilt in the refrigerator (see The Ravenwood Salad, page 134).

PROTEIN: A soft-boiled egg is perfect here, but feel free to lean on charcuterie or the last knobs of a soft cheese.

SOMETHING PICKLED: Cornichons, kimchi, sauerkraut, or pickled onions all work here.

BREAD OR CRACKERS: Add in the few lone crackers or last piece of bread in the house—toasted, if needed, drizzled with oil.

SAUCES: Mustard, chimichurri (page 140), a dollop of Tahini Green Goddess Dressing (page 223), or even your premade hummus habit (who, me?) will come in handy here.

FRUIT: Sliced apples, pears, grapes, fresh figs, plums, cherries, or dried apricots add a sweet finish. A piece of good dark chocolate wouldn't be wrong here either.

SUNDAY NIGHT DINNER

Growing up, our big Sunday meal was Swedish pancakes at the Stockholm Inn after church, where short stacks came with piles of hash browns, poached eggs, maple syrup, and lingonberry butter. While we waited for pancakes, my dad, dubbed "the Mayor," would visit with every table in the restaurant while Mom held down the fort, breaking up spoon fights and hoping no one noticed the piles of cashed-out creamer cups all over our table.

By evening, she was done enforcing manners, so we'd gather around the coffee table for Sunday night football instead. This was the *only* night of the week when we could sit on the floor, and skip napkins and forks in favor of hands and arms crossing one another, stacking cheese-and-cracker sandwiches high on paper plates.

We called this "Sunday Night Dinner," and it was everyone's favorite meal. Sunday Night Dinner was a family affair—both of my parents chipped in to pull it together, elbow to elbow in the kitchen in the late afternoon with whichever kids decided to join in. Helping was good insurance that your favorites would be in the mix, a welcome chore that didn't win an eye roll from the over-twelve set.

Anything nibbly was fair game, but the spread usually included fruits, veggies, yogurt dip, nuts, olives, summer sausage, crackers, and everyone's favorite: potted cheese. There might be something small and sweet after, like chocolate-dipped strawberries, but if a family movie was on deck, Mom would make brownies, pulling them out of the oven right before the Princess Bride escapes marriage to the wretched Prince Humperdinck.

I gather this meal came as a huge relief to my mom, who otherwise fed our family hot, from-scratch meals three times a day for two decades. I can be fairly certain, because whenever I put Sunday Night Dinner into play (which is often, especially in the summer), I have a big feeling of *ahhhh*—that floaty feeling that comes anytime you are suddenly off the hook. There's a lot to be said for a hot dinner, but there's a lot to be said for sanity, too.

In my house, Sunday Night Dinner is fair game any night of the week: whenever there are deadlines or piano lessons, or breakfast dishes still in the sink. It's my wild card—the best back-pocket meal and parenting ninja move all in one (thanks, Mom!). It doesn't have to be beautiful—in fact, unless you have company coming, keep it simple; save your time for soaking in the souls gathered around the coffee table or pillow fort with you, and piling those cheese-and-cracker sandwich stacks high. It's better than Jenga.

MAINS

BRAISED SHORT RIB SUPPER

PREP TIME: 30 MINUTES

TOTAL TIME: **3 HOURS 30 MINUTES**,
OR **8 HOURS** IN THE SLOW COOKER

SERVES **4 TO 6**

If you're going to take the time to make a proper meat-and-potatoes (or meat-and-rice) kind of dinner, make it the most melt-off-the-bone meal you can think of. This one is my favorite. I adopted this dish from my friend Chris Morocco, food editor at *Bon Appétit* and king of the simple but spectacular, the *duh* dinner you never thought of and wish you had. It's a breeze, and so big on flavor and payback, I bet it makes it into your permanent files, too.

1 onion, sliced

4 garlic cloves, smashed

¼ cup (60 ml) rice vinegar

¼ cup (60 ml) low-sodium soy sauce

2 Tbsp chopped fresh ginger

2 Tbsp coconut sugar or dark brown sugar

1 tsp red pepper flakes

3 lb (1.4 kg) beef short ribs, English (or flanken) style or Korean cut

2 cups (240 g) warm cooked basmati rice (or any favorite white rice), for serving

3 globe or watermelon radishes (or a mix), thinly sliced, for serving

Fresh cilantro leaves, for serving

If you have a slow cooker, this is its moment. Grab it, and read on.

Preheat the oven to 350°F (180°C) or prepare a 4- to 6-qt (3.5- to 5.4-L) slow cooker.

In a Dutch oven with a tight-fitting lid, or your slow cooker, combine the onion, garlic, vinegar, soy sauce, ginger, coconut sugar, red pepper flakes, and ¼ cup (60 ml) water. Add the beef and turn with tongs to coat on all sides with the sauce and onion.

Cover and cook until the beef is very tender, 2½ hours in the oven, or on low for 7 to 8 hours or on high for 5 to 6 hours in the slow cooker.

cont'd

When the meat is tender and falling off the bone, skim off and discard any excess fat, leaving the juices behind, with a ladle or spoon (skip this step if you love lots of fatty juices).

Spoon the warm rice into shallow bowls or plates. Spoon the beef and sauce over the top, and garnish with the radishes, cilantro, and all the remaining juices.

GOOD TO KNOW

Browning the beef in a little oil in the pan before cooking lends an even deeper flavor and beautiful color to your finished dish. But it's not imperative to this dish, so skip it if you're short on time.

GET AHEAD

I use a slow cooker to make the ribs while I'm out of the house. (What's better than coming home to a meal that has made itself?) Make, let cool, and refrigerate the beef in an airtight container for up to 4 days, and reheat on the stovetop over low heat. Prep the radishes hours or days ahead; refrigerate, wrapped in a damp paper towel and then zipped plastic bags, for up to 3 days. Because soft, just-cooked warm rice is always best with this meal, cook it just before serving (or use a rice cooker).

GOOD TO KNOW

To peel ginger easily, use the edge of a spoon to gently scrape away the skin, working around small creases and corners.

As a kid, I turned up my nose at meatloaf, burgers, and meatballs—anything born of ground beef. (I can't explain that one.) But one night at a cocktail party, in my twenties, a single meatball passed my way, slathered in sauce and perched on a toothpick, and I took a bite. My world was forever changed. It was moist, satisfying, unctuous.

A meatball can and should be all those things. Good meatballs satisfy on a deep level—with beef and onion and tomato creating a trifecta of flavor. Meatballs are also a brilliantly flexible make-ahead meal, refrigerator or freezer friendly at many stages, for easy dinners on the fly.

Most meatballs use a combination of beef and pork. I use grass-fed ground beef because it's easily available at my nearest supermarket, along with thick smoky bacon (aka, the pork). Sopressata and salami, often leftovers of a weekend charcuterie board, lend irresistible flavor. But don't sweat the details: As long as you mind the total weight, you can play around a little with the ratios.

Nonnas everywhere may roll over in their graves to see Manchego (a creamier Spanish cheese) rather than Parmesan in my meatballs. It lends a wonderful roundness to these luscious little meatballs, but classic Parm or pecorino works brilliantly, too.

SPAGHETTI WITH BACON AND SOPRESSATA MEATBALLS

PREP TIME: **30 MINUTES**

TOTAL TIME: **1 HOUR**

SERVES **4 TO 6**
(makes 30 to 40 small meatballs)

2 slices good-quality white bread, crusts removed

⅓ cup (80 ml) milk, warmed

2 lb (910 g) ground beef

2 slices bacon, chopped

4 thin slices sopressata, salami, or a mixture, chopped

2 garlic cloves, minced

¼ yellow onion, minced

3 large eggs, lightly beaten

¾ cup (25 g) grated Manchego or Parmesan cheese, plus more for serving

2 Tbsp chopped fresh parsley leaves

½ tsp freshly ground black pepper, plus more for serving

½ tsp flaky sea salt, such as Maldon, plus more for the sauce

2 Tbsp olive oil, plus more for the sauce

cont'd

Two 28-oz (794-g) cans whole peeled
San Marzano tomatoes

1 sprig fresh basil (optional)

Spaghetti, for serving

Soak the bread in the milk in a large bowl, turning the slices over to absorb it. Remove to a cutting board and finely chop the bread. Combine the bread, all the meats, garlic, onion, eggs, cheese, parsley, pepper, and salt in the bowl and gently mix together with clean hands until completely combined.

Shape into 1- to 2-inch (2.5- to 5-cm) meatballs, and place them on a baking sheet or platter. (Run cold water over your hands every so often, to keep the meat from sticking to your hands.) Chill the meatballs for about 10 minutes in the refrigerator while you prepare your remaining ingredients.

Heat your largest skillet or two smaller skillets over high heat. Add the oil and heat until it is shimmering, then add the meatballs in a single layer, working in batches if necessary. Fry the meatballs, letting them cook without moving them until browned on each side, for about 3 minutes per side, adding more oil to the pan if needed (tongs are great for turning the meatballs without squishing them). Remove the meatballs to a clean plate or platter.

Add the tomatoes to the pan, mashing them with a potato masher or through your fingers to break up all the large pieces; scrape the bottom of the pan to incorporate all the browned bits from the meatballs. Add the basil (if using), a pinch or two more of salt, and a glug of oil. Simmer the sauce until it is thick and flavorful, about 30 minutes.

Meanwhile, cook the spaghetti in boiling salted water until al dente.

cont'd

Return the meatballs to the sauce to warm through. Divide the spaghetti among shallow bowls or plates and spoon the sauce and meatballs over the top. Garnish with cheese and black pepper.

GET AHEAD

There are three equally reliable make-aheads for meatballs. Roll them and freeze them raw, single file on a quarter cookie sheet or plate, well wrapped, for up to 1 month. Freeze them whole and unsauced after cooking, well wrapped, for up to 2 weeks. Or cook them all the way through in the sauce, and store with the sauce in an airtight container in the refrigerator for up to 3 days.

GOOD TO KNOW

This is the one time in this book I call for minced garlic and onion, the smallest possible chop. In this case it's worth it. If needed, employ a food processor to get the job done quickly.

WHAT ELSE CAN I DO WITH MEATBALLS?

Cook and serve with broth, wilted spinach, and shaved Parmesan for a brodo soup. Smother in sauce and grated Parm or mozzarella, and serve on toasted baguettes. Skewer with small bocconcini (mozzarella balls) and serve kid-size portions on small plates. Or broil them on a lined baking sheet in the oven and serve them with mashed potatoes, lingonberries, and gravy.

When I visit my sister Jenny in Escondido, California, we always order from Lourdes, a Mexican mom-and-pop shop, my first night in town. It doesn't matter how well Lourdes makes tacos, or how much I love them—there's only one thing I want: Lourdes's chicken soup. It comes in Styrofoam containers, packed to the rim with nothing but fragrant broth and a few pieces of chicken, plus handmade tortillas, avocado halves, and heaps of lime wrapped humbly in foil. It's the perfect meal.

If you've made the whole poached chicken (page 126), this meal can be yours on the fly. Shred the chicken and add it back to the broth. Chop avocado. Toss on cilantro. Serve with lime. Perfection.

When I'm sick—but often when I'm well, too—nothing else will do.

1 poached chicken (page 126)

6 to 8 cups (about 2 L) chicken broth (page 126)

1½ to 2 tsp fine sea salt

¼ tsp freshly ground black pepper

2 firm but ripe avocados, pitted and quartered

½ cup (6 g) fresh cilantro leaves

2 to 3 limes, quartered

Warm corn tortillas or bread

Shred the chicken meat, discarding the skin and bones. Put in a large saucepan with the broth, 1½ teaspoons salt, and the pepper, and heat over low heat until warmed through, about 5 minutes. Season with additional salt to taste.

Spoon into bowls and top with the avocados and cilantro. Serve with lime for squeezing over, and warm tortillas.

ALL-SEASON CHICKEN SOUP WITH TORTILLAS AND AVOCADO

PREP TIME: 25 MINUTES

TOTAL TIME: **30 MINUTES**

SERVES **6 TO 8**

SUMMER MACARONI (NOT JUST FOR SUMMER)

PREP TIME: **10 MINUTES**

TOTAL TIME: **25 MINUTES**

SERVES **4 TO 6**

I remember the exact moment I discovered one-pot pasta, as part of a genius smart cooking story in *Martha Stewart Living* that promised perfect pasta with a sauce all in one. I sat with that image for years—a dangling carrot of ease on a long list of recipes a cookbook writer never gets around to trying while writing her own.

Meanwhile, a hundred such recipes were published, so this is an affirmation, rather than a novel discovery: One-pot pasta is real, and it's a wonder.

I finally made one when friends came for afternoon grazing and stayed, unexpectedly, for dinner. While we chatted over cheese and olives, I dashed about the kitchen throwing noodles, a sliced onion, zucchini, and a glug of olive oil into a pot. Twenty minutes and a few stirs later (that's the catch: stir, or the pasta will stick), we had a gorgeous meal.

"Is this macaroni?" my daughter asked when I brought it to the table.

"Sort of," I said. And then, more confidently: "Yes, summer macaroni!" All five kids cheered.

For the grown-ups, I topped the rest with thinly sliced radish and fresh ricotta and—as is the secret with all pasta—adequate salt. Everyone returned for seconds. So here, a friendly reminder: When it comes to feeding family or friends, ease does exist.

12 oz (340 g) chunky short pasta,
such as conchiglie, or large shells

1 sweet onion, thinly sliced

Fine sea salt

Freshly ground black pepper

1 bunch fresh lemon basil or regular basil

2 to 4 cups (150 to 300 g) chopped vegetables,
such as zucchini, kale, tomatoes, broccoli rabe,
asparagus, artichokes, and mushrooms

2 Tbsp extra-virgin olive oil

Grated Parmesan or pecorino romano,
or fresh ricotta cheese

Thinly sliced radish (optional)

cont'd

Combine the pasta, onion, 1 teaspoon salt, ½ teaspoon pepper, basil, and the chopped vegetables in a large pot with a tight-fitting lid. Add about 4½ cups (1 L) water (enough to just cover the pasta) and the oil. Cover and bring to a roaring boil. Stir, return the lid, and lower the heat to a simmer. Keep the pot covered and cook for 10 minutes, stirring every 2 minutes, until most of the liquid has been absorbed and evaporated.

Taste and add more salt and pepper as needed. Sprinkle generously with cheese and toss to coat. Serve warm, garnished with radish (if using).

GOOD TO KNOW

These ingredients are loose, and flex easily to the seasons. Many people include garlic in their one-pot-pasta. I prefer the flavor of garlic cooked in oil rather than in water, but add a few thin slices if you're a garlic lover. Other people include tomato, fresh or canned. Leave them out if you want to sell this as macaroni, but they're great in here, too. Finally, for me, this is a chunky, short noodle kind of dish, but long pasta works, too.

When life gets busy, don't forget to call on the classics—a few things that hit the right note every time and are easy to master and repeat: the kind of dinner my daughter would call *easy peasy lemon squeezy*. This is just that, and crazy delicious to boot.

24 small hard-shell clams (such as littlenecks)

Fine sea salt

2 Tbsp olive oil

4 to 6 garlic cloves, crushed

¼ tsp red pepper flakes

2½ to 3 cups (600 to 720 ml) dry white wine

1 lb (455 g) linguine

4 Tbsp (½ stick/56 g) unsalted butter, cut into cubes

½ cup (15 g) finely grated Parmesan, plus more for garnishing

⅓ cup (15 g) fresh parsley, chopped

Freshly ground black pepper

Scrub the clams clean with water and a small brush, and pick over to make sure there are no broken shells. Discard any with shells that are open or broken.

Bring a large pot of salted water to a boil. In a separate large Dutch oven or deep pot, combine the oil, garlic (4 cloves, or up to 6 if you're a garlic-loving bunch), red pepper flakes, and a pinch of salt; cook until the garlic is toasted, 1 to 2 minutes. Pour the wine over and cook until fragrant, about 2 minutes. Add the clams and continue to cook until all the clams are open, 4 to 6 minutes.

Meanwhile, cook the linguine in the boiling water until al dente, about 8 minutes. Drain and return to the pot, along with the butter, cheese, and parsley. Pour or spoon the clams and their juices over the linguine and toss well to coat. Serve warm, with more cheese and pepper.

EASY PEASY LINGUINE WITH CLAM SAUCE

PREP TIME: **10 MINUTES**

TOTAL TIME: **30 MINUTES**

SERVES **4 TO 6**

MEXICAN POLENTA BOWLS WITH ALL THE FIXINGS

PREP TIME: **10 MINUTES**

TOTAL TIME: **25 MINUTES**

SERVES **4 TO 6**

Polenta is a staple for fast, filling meals. If you buy instant polenta (and there is no shame in it) you can have a meal almost, well, instantly, just as promised. The longer-cooking kind is no more difficult, just with more standing and stirring, and it's a touch more toothsome—that's my favorite. Both have super-satisfying results, especially when topped with everyone's favorite fixings.

Set this up DIY taco bar style, with bowls of shredded cheese, sliced scallions, warm black beans, chopped avocados, wedges of lime, and anything else you love on a taco or burrito.

2 cups (480 ml) whole milk

¾ tsp fine sea salt

1 cup (140 g) polenta

2 Tbsp unsalted butter (optional)

2 oz (55 g) sharp white Cheddar, Manchego, or Monterey Jack cheese, shredded

TOPPINGS

1½ cups (240 g) Easy Smoky Black Beans (page 148), warmed

2 ripe avocados, chopped

Shredded cheese

Fresh pico de gallo, salsa, or Basil-Poblano-Garlic Relish (page 85)

1 lime, cut into wedges

Flaky sea salt, such as Maldon

Combine the milk, 1 cup (240 ml) water, and salt in a large saucepan over medium-high heat. Bring to a roaring boil and gradually whisk in the polenta. Cook, stirring occasionally, over medium-low heat until no lumps remain, about 10 minutes.

Remove from the heat and vigorously stir in the butter (if using) and cheese until all is melted. Spoon the warm polenta into four shallow bowls and add the toppings to your liking. Serve with lime wedges, flaky salt, and a good Mexican beer.

GET AHEAD
Prep all your garnish ingredients up to 1 day ahead and refrigerate, well wrapped, for a fast weeknight meal that comes together in minutes.

GOOD TO KNOW
White or brown rice works as the base of this tacoless taco bowl, too.

WHITE RISOTTO WITH CORN, CARROTS, AND KALE

PREP TIME: **15 MINUTES**

TOTAL TIME: **1 HOUR**

SERVES **4**

When we lived in New York City, we had a farmers' market half a block from our front steps. Every Wednesday, we'd stroll down the block with Greta and let her pick three vegetables for dinner that night. Her combinations were good challenges for my cooking muscle. When summer slipped into fall one cool morning, we brought home corn, kale, and young purple carrots, and this dish was born.

Risotto is the ultimate comfort food—warm and filling—and when it comes right down to it, easier than most of us believe. Make this with your favorite vegetables in any season, adding more if you're a veggie-centric sort, or less if you want mostly soothing rice. The white risotto combo (onion, rice, white wine, Parm) is a classic and morphs readily to your whim.

2 Tbsp extra-virgin olive oil, plus more for cooking vegetables

1 onion, finely chopped

2 cups (400 g) Arborio rice

⅔ cup (160 ml) dry white wine

5 to 5½ cups (1.2 to 1.3 L) chicken broth (page 126) or water, warm

Fine sea salt

Freshly ground black pepper

4 Tbsp (½ stick/56 g) unsalted butter

1 bunch young heirloom carrots (about 6), trimmed and scrubbed, halved lengthwise

½ bunch (45 g) Tuscan kale, larger leaves torn or cut into pieces (about 3 cups)

2 ears corn, kernels cut from the cob

½ cup (15 g) grated Parmesan cheese, plus more coarsely grated for garnish

Heat the oil in a heavy saucepan or Dutch oven over medium-high heat. Add the onion and cook, stirring, until soft and translucent, about 3 minutes. Add the rice and stir to coat with the oil. Stir in the wine and cook until the wine has evaporated, 1 minute more.

Stir in 2 cups (480 ml) of the warm broth and salt and pepper to taste, and bring to a boil. Stir, reduce the heat to medium-low, and cook until the liquid has

cont'd

evaporated. Add ½ cup (120 ml) of the broth and continue stirring, adding more broth ½ cup (120 ml) at a time, until the liquid has evaporated and the rice is al dente, 20 to 25 minutes. Most of the liquid should be absorbed and the rice just cooked, with about ½ cup (120 ml) broth remaining.

While the rice cooks, heat another 1 tablespoon oil and 1 tablespoon of the butter in a large skillet over medium-low heat. Add the carrots and brown slightly. Add enough water to come about one-third of the way up the carrots and cook until just fork tender, but still deep in color. Add the kale and stir to wilt, 5 minutes more. Add the corn and cook until the kernels turn bright yellow but are still crisp, 1 minute more. Season the vegetables well and use a slotted spoon to remove them from the liquid.

Stir in another ½ cup (120 ml) broth to the risotto as needed; add the remaining 3 tablespoons butter and the cheese and stir. Stir in the vegetables, or serve the risotto in bowls topped with the warm vegetables and coarsely grated Parmesan.

GET AHEAD

Though risotto should always be served fresh and hot from the stove, when it is creamy, you can stop risotto midway, before your rice is cooked through. Cook just until the rice is soft on the outside, but still firm in the middle, about 10 minutes. Remove it from the heat and transfer it to a plate to cool (or, if you're in a hurry, set the pan down outside, covered, on a cool day to stop the cooking). Cover with plastic wrap and let it hang out at room temperature for up to 8 hours. When you're ready to eat, jump back in where you left off, adding warm broth, until the rice is cooked through and creamy throughout. As always, prep and refrigerate your vegetables in an airtight container for up to 2 days.

BAKED FISH WITH CHERRY TOMATOES, CAPERS, AND HERBS

PREP TIME: **10 MINUTES**

TOTAL TIME: **30 MINUTES**

SERVES **4**

This may be the easiest dinner you'll ever make. It relies on the innate deliciousness of fresh fish, and the magic that happens when it bathes in olive oil and lemon and capers while it cooks. The only thing you need to know how to do here is shop well (buy the best fish you can find; almost any meaty white fish will work) and how to turn on your oven; the rest is pure arrive-at-the-table-and-enjoy ease.

Four 4- to 6-oz (115- to 170-g) fillets meaty white fish, such as halibut, cod, grouper, or mackerel

¼ cup (60 ml) olive oil

1 heaping pint (280 g) cherry or grape tomatoes, on or off the vine

One 2-oz (56-g) jar capers, drained

2 garlic cloves, sliced

1½ tsp flaky sea salt, such as Maldon

Freshly ground black pepper

1 lemon, cut into wedges

Fresh herbs, such as thyme or oregano

Preheat the oven to 400°F (200°C).

Arrange the fish in a small baking pan (about 7 by 11 inches/17 by 28 cm) or a 9-inch (23-cm) ovenproof skillet and drizzle the oil over the top. Turn the fish once to coat, and scatter the tomatoes, capers (half a jar, or all of it if you're caper lovers), garlic, salt, and pepper evenly over the fish. Toss in the lemon wedges.

Roast until the tomatoes give off some of their juices and wilt, and the fish is just cooked through, 20 to 30 minutes depending on the thickness of the fish.

Remove from the oven and scatter the herbs over the fish. Serve warm, dividing the fish and toppings among serving plates, and squeeze the roasted lemon over the top before eating.

ABOUT THE FISH IN MY PURSE

In my twenties, I went to culinary school at night, after my day job curating photos for an art magazine. I decided to do it that way because, I reasoned, if I didn't mind missing out on nightlife to go to class three times a week, I'd know I was serious about cooking.

One night I met some friends out after class with a large, fresh Dover sole in my purse—an extra from class. When I arrived, I slipped into an empty seat at the bar, and asked the barman if he could kindly stow my fish for an hour or two. Barmen are never short on ice. His eyebrows raised, then he cracked a smile. Done.

The next day, the friends enjoyed a whole roasted sole with lemon, browned butter, and capers; they were silent, slurping up every bite. Still, I'll never hear the end about the night I brought a fish to a bar.

I'm shameless in the pursuit of good food. I almost never travel without snacks (whole olives, smoked almonds, 78% dark chocolate) or fresh kale in my carry-on, yanked from the garden in case, you know, our only option for dinner is airport pizza (instructions: add kale, fold pizza, eat). I always have a small tin of Maldon salt for emergency seasoning, and I bring herbs instead of flowers to dinner parties.

My point: It's okay for you to be a little shameless in your pursuit of good food, too. People are fanatical about all kinds of ridiculous things—their yoga pants, their coffee, their lap dogs. Don't apologize because you no longer eat meat or recently shed gluten, or because you always eat dessert even if no one else does. Maybe you ran five miles today! Or maybe not. Whatever the case, not everyone will get it, but I do. Eat what makes you feel alive and helps you know that you're living your very best life.

Someday, you'll thank yourself.

Most groceries have a juicy, already roasted chicken you can buy and shred into tacos, quesadillas, chicken salad, chicken soup, enchiladas, and more. It's an easy dinner solve, the kind of recommendation food editors (like me) have been making for decades. But just as easy—hear me out—and more delicious, is making a whole bird at home. You can control the quality (Organic? Amish? Kosher?) and benefit from tender, juicy chicken that can morph into a handful of memorable meals all week.

Poaching a bird whole is genius: You get plenty of juicy meat (the easy-shredding kind) plus a fragrant broth—which is an instant base for some of the best soups in this book. If make-ahead is your MO, this technique is all you.

THE JUICIEST WHOLE BIRD (AND BROTH)

PREP TIME: **15 MINUTES**

TOTAL TIME: **1 HOUR 30 MINUTES**

SERVES **4 TO 6** (makes 13 cups/3.1 L broth, plus 7 cups/945 g shredded chicken)

1 knob fresh ginger, peeled

3 scallions, halved, or a bunch of parsley stems, tied with twine

1 Tbsp toasted sesame or peanut oil

1 head of garlic, unpeeled, halved

One 4-lb (1.8-kg) chicken

1 Tbsp fine sea salt

Five 1-qt (1-L) containers with tight-fitting lids

Combine the ginger, scallions, sesame oil, garlic, and 16 cups (4 L) water in a large pot over high heat and bring to a boil. Meanwhile, rub the chicken all over with the salt and set it aside until the water boils. Slip the chicken gently into the water, breast side down, and return the water to a boil. Lower the heat to medium and simmer for 20 minutes. Remove from the heat, cover the pot tightly with a lid, and allow the chicken to stand in the hot water for 1 hour (the chicken will cook through, but gently).

Lift the chicken from the broth and set aside. Strain out the ginger, scallions, and garlic, reserving the broth, or use a slotted spoon to pull them out and discard. Taste the broth and season to your liking with more salt or sesame oil. (I find that the toasted sesame oil is subtle, but it rounds out the broth beautifully.) Use the broth while it's hot, or let cool completely, then pour into three 1-qt (1-L) containers.

Pull the skin off the chicken and discard. Cut the chicken into large pieces, off the bone, or use your fingers to pull all of the meat off the bones into lovely big chunks (you can shred it later, as needed). Serve warm, or let cool and refrigerate, in two 1-qt (1-L) containers, for up to 3 days. Often, if I know it's destined for soup, I store the chicken in the broth, to keep it super moist.

COOKI
FOR
FRIEND

PIZZA NIGHT

SPRING ONION AND SALAMI SHEET-PAN PIZZA

PREP TIME: **10 MINUTES**

TOTAL TIME: **35 MINUTES**

SERVES **8**

Where I grew up, the only acceptable pizza was a deep-dish Chicago-style cheese fest. I didn't achieve true pizza nirvana until I moved to New York, home of thin-crust pies scattered with farmers' market loot at places like Roberta's in Brooklyn and Milkflower in Queens—meccas for family meetups with friends.

We've since moved to another thin-crust pizza wasteland (except for glorious summer evenings at Westwind Orchard), but we still crave a pizza-night kind of affair: inexpensive, casual hangouts with friends that leave everyone satisfied, but not stuffed. The solution: making pizza at home. I'm no pizza wizard, so I embraced the deep-dish (or grandma-style) pie of my youth, only sexier (with nowhere near as much cheese).

For the adults, this spicy, fennel and spicy sausage moment wins raves. A simpler cheese and broccoli version keeps small people happy—and parents satisfied with the just-enough-vegetables vibe to let you kick back and feel you've done your job (use sweet Italian sausage only, and replace the fennel with broccoli, one for one).

¼ cup (60 ml) olive oil, plus extra for drizzling

Two 1-lb (455-g) balls multigrain or plain pizza dough, at room temperature (see note, page 132)

1 cup All-Purpose Red Sauce (page 133)

2½ cups (12 oz/200 g) shredded mozzarella cheese

4 oz (115 g) salami, sopressata, or Italian sausage

1 small spring onion or fennel bulb, thinly sliced

½ tsp fennel seeds, crushed (optional)

½ cup (about 2 oz/15 g) finely grated Parmesan or pecorino romano cheese

Flaky sea salt, such as Maldon

Fresh baby greens or herbs

Position a rack in the lower third of the oven and preheat to 525°F (275°C). (If your oven only goes to 500°F/260°C, that's fine.)

cont'd

Coat a 13 by 18 inch (33 by 46 cm) baking sheet with the oil. Gently stretch the two balls of dough into an even layer, to reach into all four corners of the baking sheet, taking your time to stretch evenly with the seam meeting in the middle. Press the seam together to make one large sheet of dough. Spoon the tomato sauce evenly over the top, sprinkle with the mozzarella, and top with salami, spring onion, fennel seeds (if using), and Parmesan.

Bake until crisp and brown on the bottom and around the edges, about 25 minutes. Remove from the oven and sprinkle with flaky salt. Top with the greens and drizzle lightly with more oil. Serve warm.

GOOD TO KNOW

I've made this pizza with corn and grated zucchini, salami and green olives, red onion and shaved winter squash. Anything goes. The sauce and onions are the only musts; just avoid anything too wet that will make your crust soggy because the oven is super hot and the cook time is short.

LET'S TALK PIZZA DOUGH

Sometimes I make my own pizza dough, but for this kind of pizza, which doesn't have to stretch ultra-thin, the multigrain pizza dough from the supermarket, or dough from our local pizza shop, does the trick perfectly. The key is to let it set at room temperature for a good long while—at least an hour—so it is warm and puffy, and takes to stretching onto the baking sheet like a dream.

ALL-PURPOSE RED SAUCE

TOTAL TIME: **5 MINUTES**
SERVES **8**

Some people are picky about the difference between pizza sauce, pasta sauce, and marinara. I don't have time to be. I like my tomato sauce pure, tasty, and just seasoned enough (read: not sweet, not salty), just shy of *cooked*, so you can still taste the life in every tomato. For pizza, I puree this sauce raw in a food processor or blender, then spoon it on the dough, where it will cook in the oven. For pasta, I add the same ingredients to a shallow pan (without draining the tomatoes) and simmer for about 20 minutes, then spoon it chunky over my noodles—though it's fine to puree it for pasta, too. In no time, you'll learn exactly how to make red sauce work for you.

One 28-oz (794-g) can whole peeled tomatoes
(such as San Marzano), drained

2 anchovy fillets packed in oil, drained (optional)

2 garlic cloves

6 Tbsp (90 ml) olive oil

¼ cup (3 g) fresh basil leaves

Pinch of red pepper flakes (optional)

Fine sea salt

Freshly ground black pepper

Pulse the tomatoes, anchovies (if using), garlic, oil, and basil in a food processor or blender until mostly smooth (some texture is okay); season with red pepper flakes (if using), salt, and pepper.

Serve Flourless Chocolate Brownie Cake (page 167) for dessert.

THE RAVENWOOD SALAD

TOTAL TIME: **20 MINUTES**

SERVES **6 TO 8**

Everyone needs a killer side dish, hearty but refreshing, that can be made ahead and served at any occasion, any time of the year—the kind of thing you can equally bring to a potluck or serve on an elegant spread. This is it.

Top chef in our crowd is Chris Lanier and his partner, Dana McClure, founders of Ravenwood, a food and design haven in upstate New York. At one of our gatherings, they showed up with a salad no one could stop eating—a *kale salad* that outshone all the cookies, brownies, and house-cured sausages on the spread combined. Because I love you, I asked for the recipe and their permission to include it here. It goes with absolutely everything, especially sheet-pan pizza (page 130), Magic Pork Shoulder (page 157), or roast chicken (page 136).

As for the specifics, there's lots of flexibility. Just don't skimp on the cheese. That's the Ravenwood way.

RAVENWOOD DRESSING

⅔ cup (160 ml) extra-virgin olive oil

⅓ cup (80 ml) red wine vinegar

1 Tbsp Dijon mustard

1 tsp honey

Freshly ground black pepper

RAVENWOOD SALAD

½ cup (70 g) sunflower seeds

½ cup (70 g) pepitas (hulled pumpkin seeds)

¼ cup (60 ml) olive oil

Flaky sea salt, such as Maldon

1 bunch kale (curly or lacinato), torn into small pieces or thinly sliced

½ head radicchio, thinly sliced

¼ head green cabbage, shredded or thinly sliced

2 large carrots, grated or thinly sliced

½ red onion, thinly sliced

½ cup (15 g) finely grated Parmesan cheese

Preheat the oven to 350°F (180°C).

TO MAKE THE DRESSING: Whisk together the oil, vinegar, mustard, honey, and pepper until smooth (or blend in a blender).

TO MAKE THE SALAD: Toss the sunflower seeds and pepitas in the oil and flaky salt to taste, and spread out on a baking sheet. Roast in the oven until lightly golden and fragrant, 5 to 8 minutes; do not let them burn—they shouldn't be dark.

Layer the dressing, toasted seeds, and then the greens and vegetables in a large bowl. Top with the cheese. Cover tightly and refrigerate until ready to serve, up to overnight. Before serving, toss together. Taste and add more salt, if needed, and serve at room temperature.

CHICKEN AND OYSTERS

―――――

ROAST CHICKEN (PARTS) WITH LEMON AND GREEN OLIVES

PREP TIME: **10 MINUTES**

TOTAL TIME: **35 MINUTES**

SERVES **4 TO 8**

Sometimes we need a dinner for friends that screams "fall"—something cozy and simple, but still special. Roast chicken always does the trick.

This recipe is as simple to make as it is to serve; chicken parts mean no carving, and everybody scoops up the meat—breast, thigh, leg—they most enjoy. It works equally well with capers and oranges, or black olives and lemons; you get the idea. You want something salty and briny to flavor the bird, and something bright and citric to finish.

For an easy, autumnal meal, start with wine and oysters, and serve with the brilliant and seasonless staple Ravenwood salad (page 134) alongside.

1 chicken, cut into 6 pieces

1 tsp fine sea salt

Freshly ground black pepper

3 Tbsp olive oil

1 lemon, cut into wedges

⅓ cup (45 g) Castelvetrano or Cerignola olives (unpitted or pitted)

Preheat the oven to 450°F (230°C) with the rack in the upper third. Arrange the chicken pieces on a rimmed baking sheet or in a 9 by 13 inch (23 by 33 cm) baking pan. Season generously with salt and pepper and let sit, uncovered, at room temperature while the oven preheats. (If you have the time, you can season it and let it rest overnight, uncovered, in the refrigerator before cooking, for crispiest skin.)

Drizzle the chicken with the oil and toss the lemon wedges and olives over it. Roast until the chicken is deep golden brown, some fat has cooked off, and the juices run clear, about 30 minutes. Serve warm, or let cool and refrigerate in an airtight container for up to 3 days or in the freezer for up to 2 weeks.

CRAZY SIMPLE SUMMER SUPPER

GRILLED SKIRT STEAK WITH CHIMICHURRI

PREP TIME: **15 MINUTES**

TOTAL TIME: **30 MINUTES**

SERVES **6**

Few things are better at herding a summer crowd than a tender steak, grilled to perfection, doused with a potent, garlic-laced chimichurri. My go-to side for this main event is a big tomato salad, or caprese, also simpler than simple. The natural endnote to this drop-dead simple meal is watermelon, of course, and ice cream—store bought. Keep it simple so the focus can be on good company and conversation.

4 lb (1.8 kg) skirt steak

2 packed cups (24 g) fresh flat-leaf parsley leaves, chopped

⅔ cup (160 ml) extra-virgin olive oil, plus more for the grill

6 Tbsp (90 ml) fresh lemon juice

2 garlic cloves, pressed or minced

1 to 2 tsp red pepper flakes

Flaky sea salt, such as Maldon

Freshly ground black pepper

Preheat the grill or a grill pan to medium-high and lightly oil it. Remove the steak from the refrigerator and let it sit out while you preheat the grill, 20 minutes.

Toss together the parsley, oil, lemon juice, garlic, red pepper flakes, salt, and pepper to taste. Set aside. (You can make this up to 2 hours in advance.)

Season the steak on both sides generously with salt and pepper. Grill until the meat is charred and medium-rare inside, about 2 minutes per side. Transfer to a cutting board and let rest without touching the steak for 5 minutes (don't rush this—the secret is keeping the juicy flavor *inside* the steak). Slice the steak across the grain, transfer to a serving platter, and scatter the chimichurri all over the top.

WINTER CHEESE (AND ANY VEGETABLE) BRUNCH STRATA

PREP TIME: **20 MINUTES**

TOTAL TIME: **1 HOUR**

SERVES **8**

Strata is a force: a gooey, savory bread pudding with all the flavor, all the fat, and all the guilt. But forget all the guilt. It's so darn good and totally worth it. Plus, you can toss the bread and egg custard together in advance, plunk it in the refrigerator, and then bake it fresh in the morning for a crowd.

This is the thing I make to feed overnight guests, especially in the fall and winter, before we go out for a romp in the elements to burn it all off again.

8 thick slices (about 6 cups/130 g) hearty ciabatta bread

6 large eggs, lightly beaten

3 cups (720 ml) whole milk

1¼ cups (5 oz/140 g) shredded Gruyère cheese

Fine sea salt

Freshly ground black pepper

3 to 4 slices thick-cut bacon, cooked and torn (optional)

2 cups (300 g) chopped cooked vegetables, such as spinach, mushrooms, or poblano peppers

Butter a 9 by 13 inch (23 by 33 cm) ceramic baking dish. Cut the bread into cubes. Scatter over the prepared dish.

Whisk together the eggs and milk. Stir in half of the cheese, and season with salt and pepper. Pour three-quarters of the egg mixture over the bread cubes. Layer the bacon over the bread and scatter the vegetables over the entire dish. Pour the remaining egg mixture over the vegetables and top with the remaining cheese. Cover with plastic wrap and refrigerate overnight.

In the morning, preheat the oven to 350°F (180°C).

Remove the plastic wrap and bake the strata until just set—a quarter-size wobbly part in the center is perfect, but the rest should feel set—40 to 50 minutes.

Let the strata cool, about 20 minutes or longer. Cut or scoop into portions and serve warm or at room temperature, with a large salad.

MAKE-AHEAD BRUNCH FOR A CROWD

BITTER GREENS AND BEETS SALAD

TOTAL TIME: **25 MINUTES**

SERVES **6 TO 8**

This bracing citrus salad is the perfect accompaniment to anything meaty, fatty, cheesy, gooey, bready, or otherwise deliciously decadent. It has all the right notes to give you a good, clean finish to the whole meal. I serve it for brunch with strata, alongside pizza (page 130), and of course with pasta and Sunday Sauce (page 212). At its essence, this salad lives beautifully with Italian food, but it's welcome at any meal—especially brunch.

2 Tbsp extra-virgin olive oil

1 Tbsp sherry vinegar or apple cider vinegar

Freshly ground black pepper

1 small head radicchio or Treviso

½ bulb fennel, trimmed and thinly sliced

¼ cup (3 g) fresh flat-leaf parsley leaves

¼ cup (3 g) celery leaves

3 golden or red beets, trimmed, cooked, and sliced

2 small oranges or clementines, peeled and sliced

Toasted hazelnuts, peeled

½ tsp flaky sea salt, such as Maldon

Whisk together the oil, vinegar, and pepper in the bottom of a large bowl. Layer in the remaining ingredients, radicchio first. Cover and refrigerate until ready to serve. Just before serving, toss the salad together and season with salt.

GET AHEAD

This recipe is a great get-ahead dish because the crispy vegetables can withstand sitting on top of the dressing before tossing for several hours. If you love this combination, make these salads in one- or two-serving portions in jars or glass containers, and refrigerate overnight for workday lunches, too.

ALL-OCCASION TACO FEAST

Whether we're feeding four friends or fourteen, meat-eaters or vegetarians, we always know we can count on this menu, which you'll find in varying forms at our table all year long. It can be based on the Magic Pork Shoulder (page 157) or the Fish Contramar (page 152), or you can absolutely make it a simple rice-and-beans affair. Improvise where you see fit—but don't skip this indispensable tomatillo sauce. It couldn't be simpler or more perfect for quesadillas, fish tacos, and flank steak dinners. Adults and kids alike douse their dinner plate; it works on the pork, atop simple rice and beans, or alongside the sweet, tender plantains. There's never, ever leftovers.

SPICY TOMATILLO–LIME SAUCE

PREP TIME: **15 MINUTES**

TOTAL TIME: **30 MINUTES**

SERVES **16** (makes 4 cups/960 ml)

10 tomatillos (about 1¾ lb/829 g), husks removed

2 serrano peppers, left whole

1 yellow onion, quartered

1 bunch fresh cilantro, leaves and stems (about 4 packed cups/48 g)

1½ tsp fine sea salt

2 Tbsp extra-virgin olive oil

1 Tbsp fresh lime juice

1 Tbsp honey

Preheat the oven to broil (high), with the rack on the top third.

Arrange the tomatillos, peppers, and onion quarters on a rimmed baking sheet. Broil until the tomatillos are soft and browned, 15 to 20 minutes, turning with tongs halfway through cooking. Let cool. Transfer the vegetables, with any of their liquid, to a blender along with the cilantro, ½ cup (120 ml) water, the salt, oil, lime juice, and honey, and process until smooth. Set aside, covered, until ready to serve.

EASY SMOKY BLACK BEANS

TOTAL TIME: **15 MINUTES**

SERVES **8**

Two 15.5-oz (439-g) cans low-sodium black beans, rinsed and drained

2 Tbsp olive oil

½ tsp fine sea salt

¼ tsp smoked paprika

¼ cup (60 ml) fresh lime juice

In a saucepan, heat the beans, ¼ cup (60 ml) water, the oil, salt, and paprika over medium-low heat until warm and saucy. Just before serving, add the lime juice; serve warm.

SHALLOW-FRIED PLANTAINS

PREP TIME: **10 MINUTES**

TOTAL TIME: **30 MINUTES**

SERVES **8**

⅓ cup (75 g) coconut oil

4 very ripe plantains, sliced crosswise or lengthwise

Flaky sea salt, such as Maldon

Preheat a griddle or cast-iron pan over medium-high heat.

Heat 2 tablespoons of the oil on the griddle, add the plantains in batches, and cook until golden on one side and starting to soften, about 6 minutes. Flip and continue cooking until golden and evenly soft throughout, 4 to 6 minutes more. Sprinkle with salt and serve warm. Repeat with the remaining plantains.

GET AHEAD

I make the tomatillo-lime sauce about once a month, right after a grocery trip. Before you unpack, husk the tomatillos, quarter an onion, and get them both under the broiler along with the peppers. They will roast, soften, and cool in a flash while you put groceries away. Pack up any extras in a jar with a tight-fitting lid, and top off with olive oil (to keep the sauce bright green). Refrigerate, in an airtight container, for up to 1 week, for freeze for up to 1 month.

GOOD TO KNOW

You can amp up the heat and punch on the tomatillo-lime sauce to your family's liking by tweaking the number of peppers (or using jalapeños for milder spice).

CANNED BEANS

Yes, canned beans are considered a cheat by some (even my former self), but hallelujah, they're so easy to make into a quick, delicious side for this feast. Look for organic, low-sodium beans.

FISH CONTRAMAR

TOTAL TIME: **40 MINUTES**
SERVES **6**

On our honeymoon, András and I spent a few nights in Mexico City on our way to the surfing villages along Mexico's southern coast. Our first meal was at Contramar, a Mexico City must. We rode borrowed bikes from our hotel in the Condesa straight there on our first day, and ordered the fish Contramar: a whole snapper smothered with a red chile sauce on one half and a parsley sauce on the other. I still dream about that meal.

After that trip, I made this dish for parties, always to great acclaim; it's smart and easy. I'm probably not the first person to have introduced you to Fish Contramar, or the last, but I'm including it here because it's an easy swap-out for the Magic Pork Shoulder (page 157) if fish is more your thing for a taco feast. You can serve many of the same sides—the tortillas and limes are the most important—plus a batch of pickled white onions. They're perfect with the fish.

For a big crowd, you can serve both the pork and the fish—which satisfies in the *every delicious option* category. But know that you can spread these sauces on smaller fillets for just a few folks, too.

RED CHILE SAUCE

4 dried red chiles, like casabel or pasilla, seeds removed

1 ancho chile, seeds removed

2 dried chiles de árbol

1 plum tomato, cored

½ small yellow onion

5 garlic cloves, peeled

⅓ cup (80 ml) vegetable oil

2 Tbsp fresh orange juice

1 Tbsp fresh lime juice

¼ tsp ground cumin

Fine sea salt to taste

cont'd

PARSLEY SAUCE

4 garlic cloves, peeled

2 packed cups (25 g) fresh parsley leaves and stems

⅓ cup (80 ml) vegetable oil

Pinch of ground cumin

Fine sea salt to taste

FISH

1 whole red snapper fillet, or one 2-lb (910-g) piece of halibut, pin bones removed

Fine sea salt

Freshly ground black pepper

Pickled white onions (page 226), warmed corn tortillas, quartered avocados, and lime wedges, for serving

TO MAKE THE RED CHILE SAUCE: Put all the dried chiles in a medium saucepan with enough water to cover; bring to a simmer. Cover the pan, remove from the heat, and let sit for 30 minutes to soften. Drain.

Combine the steeped chiles, tomato, onion, garlic, oil, orange juice, lime juice, and cumin in a blender, and puree to a chunky paste. Taste and season with salt; set aside, covered, until ready to use.

TO MAKE THE PARSLEY SAUCE: In a clean blender jar, puree the garlic, parsley, oil, and cumin until mostly smooth. Taste and season with salt; set aside, covered, until ready to use.

TO MAKE THE FISH: Preheat a grill to medium; brush the grates with oil. Pat the fish dry on both sides with paper towels and use a sharp knife to score the flesh side with cuts about ¼ inch (6 mm) thick and 1 inch (2.5 cm) apart, on the diagonal. Season generously with salt and pepper. Spread the chile sauce on half of the fillet and the parsley sauce on the other. (Contramar spreads it lengthwise, but I put the parsley sauce on the wider portion of the fillet, since that always goes first in my crowd.)

Grill the fish, skin side down (a large halibut fillet may be skinless), until the skin is crispy and the fish is almost cooked through, 8 to 10 minutes, depending on the thickness of the fish. Flip the fish carefully and just kiss the coated side on the grill, until it releases easily, about 2 minutes. Serve the fish flesh side up on a warm platter, with pickled onions, tortillas, avocados, and limes.

GET AHEAD
Make the two sauces and store them in airtight containers in the refrigerator for up to 1 day (the parsley will lose color, so top with oil to prevent air from reaching it).

Good to Know

An 8-pound (3.6-kg) shoulder easily feeds 10 to 12 adults plus a handful of small kids as a taco filling. For a smaller group, use a 4- to 6-pound (1.8- to 2.7-kg) shoulder instead, reducing the cook time a bit and halving the spice rub. Use a whole bottle of beer, regardless.

Get Ahead

Cook this dish completely ahead; cool, wrap tightly, and keep in the refrigerator, in the braising liquid, for up to 5 days, or in the freezer for up to 1 month. Reheat slowly in a large Dutch oven over low heat. (If frozen, bring to room temperature before warming.)

MAGIC PORK SHOULDER

PREP TIME: **25 MINUTES**

TOTAL TIME: **8 HOURS**
(+ 1 DAY TO MARINATE; OPTIONAL)

SERVES: **10 TO 12**

I married a vegetarian and didn't eat meat for a
good long while. We had a first kid, then a second,
moved to the country, and got our first serious dining
room table—in rapid succession. House with a big
table and kids begets dozens of parties for holidays,
birthdays, and merry making. For a long time, I served
vegetarian entrées to everyone who came, no matter
what they ate at home. But one day I slow-braised a
big old pork shoulder for the meat-eaters.

The house filled and people raved. So, I did it
again.

Without realizing it, a braised pork shoulder
became my party meat. I'd make loads of roast vegetables and homemade tortillas, rice and beans, baked
plantains, and some kind of potent green sauce (page
220) for everyone, then slow-braise a pork shoulder
for the meat-eaters.

By instinct, I sent the extras home with the
meat-eaters. And then one day, I kept a little back
for the kids. The benefits of having tender, succulent
pork meat by the pound on the stove, and later in
the refrigerator (or the freezer) rewarded us tenfold.
I could heat up a little to serve with warm mashed
potatoes. I could use a little to top a rice bowl, or
stuff it into burritos with shredded lettuce and beans.

Gradually I started seeing just how deliciously
convenient this new habit was. In fact, it was virtually
magic. The meat was always moist and tender, and
there was only one big pot to clean for weeks' worth
of food. It wasn't something we would eat every day,
or even every week, but something that, when we did, I
was proud to have made.

If you want real magic—make this in a slow
cooker or Instant Pot, where the long cook time doesn't
determine whether or not you can stay at home all
day. Either way you go, make this if you have any plans
in sight to feed the masses. They. Will. Rave.

cont'd

2 Tbsp brown sugar

1 Tbsp smoked paprika

2 tsp fine sea salt

1 tsp freshly ground black pepper

1 tsp cayenne pepper

1 tsp fennel seeds

One 8½-lb (about 4-kg) bone-in pork shoulder (Boston butt)

One 12-oz (360-ml) bottle flavorful beer (*not* a light beer)

Pickled vegetables (page 226), warmed corn tortillas, quartered avocados, and lime wedges, for serving

Combine the brown sugar, paprika, salt, black pepper, cayenne, and fennel in a small bowl. Place the pork in a large bowl and rub the spices all over, being sure to cover all sides. Wrap well and refrigerate for at least 1 hour and up to overnight. Bring the pork to room temperature on the countertop for 1 hour before roasting.

Preheat the oven to 450°F (230°C).

Put the seasoned pork in a large Dutch oven, fat side up, and roast, uncovered, until lightly browned, 45 minutes. Pour the beer over the pork, lower the oven temperature to 300°F (150°C), and cover the pot. Cook until the pork is completely tender and pulls easily from the bone, about 6 hours.

Remove from the oven. Transfer the pork to a plate and remove the bone. Cook the liquid over medium-high heat until slightly reduced, about 15 minutes. (I often skip this part because the liquid cooks down every time I reheat the leftover pork all week long.) Meanwhile, shred the pork, using two forks. Let the liquid cool slightly, then return the pork to the liquid to keep warm. Serve warm, with all the goodies.

COMPANY
CHICKEN

————————

When I was a kid, my mom made a dish called Company Chicken, only when company came. It was a casserole of chicken breasts and dried beef smothered in creamy mushroom soup (canned, thank you). It was rich and filling, and not in the least bit beautiful, but no one minded. That was before Instagram.

Her other go-to dish for guests was Cheesy Chicken Casserole: a tangled mass of angel hair pasta loaded with melted cheese. You knew it was good—and not just to us—because if Mom served buffet style, there was a pile-up of repeat guests at the front of the line. They knew: Cheesy Chicken Casserole went fast.

She strayed from these classics rarely. One night, when I was in high school, my boyfriend, a towering pro-bound linebacker, came to dinner at our house for the first time. That night my mom served salmon loaf.

"Mom, salmon loaf?" I remember my brother saying. My mom, ever gracious, just smiled, and heaped a generous portion on the boyfriend's plate. He claimed to love it. The rest of us spent 30 minutes scooching it around our plates with our forks. After that, Mom went straight back to Company Chicken, and we were glad.

Later, as a freshly minted New Yorker, I befriended a charming woman famous for hosting a rotating cast of friends for frequent, intimate dinners. At my first one, she presented a steaming antique tureen, filled with creamed soup, and freshly baked bread. For the main course, she served bobotie—minced onions and lamb, buried in a rich custard coating—the signature dish of her native South Africa. Each time I returned, I sat down to the same meal, with a textbook exactness, footed tureen and all. But I'd come to expect and hope for it; just like Mom's Company Chicken, it was that delicious thing we could count on.

Somewhere in the business of writing hundreds of recipes, I'd forgotten about Company Chicken and bobotie. I've hardly had the luxury of a repeat performer. Most days I'm testing new recipes—often on deadline—so when company comes, I improvise and throw a few wild cards into the mix. It always works, but, in retrospect, maybe it was missing something—something familiar.

Eventually, we moved out of the city and my circle expanded again, this time to include my (now) dear friend Rebecca. A consummate host, Rebecca is an exacting user of recipes, noting any tweaks to perfect her successes again and again. When my son was born, she fed us often. She'd hold him (so I could eat two-handed!), refill my plate, and pour us tea. One memorable night Rebecca made ricotta cake, casually streaked with raspberries and chocolate chips. It looked like art, and tasted like heaven. We both ate two slices (as all best girlfriends do).

After that night, she made that cake again and again. I think of that year in our friendship as the Year of the Raspberry Ricotta Cake. When it fell off her radar, I mourned its loss. But as her cake slipped away, new, comforting favorites emerged: Frida's chocolate-clad Sarah Bernhardt cookies, Tait's chewy sourdough, Kyle's heap of briny oysters, and Catherine's dense, chocolaty hedgehog cake (yes, hedgehog).

Meanwhile, I found my own repeat performers. For my kids' birthdays, I make Magic Pork Shoulder (page 157) and Spicy Tomatillo-Lime Sauce (page 146). Everyone knows it will be there, along with warm tortillas and pickled onions and soft, sweet plantains. For baby showers, I make Easier-than-Pie Warm Apple Tart (It's True) (page 188) or Almost-Famous Cranberry Bundt Cake (page 164); both travel well and my girl posse loves them. For the intimates who help keep our two small businesses running during our busiest times, I make Sunday Sauce (page 212) and tiramisu (page 176), and send everyone home with enough for tomorrow, too.

That's how I knew it was time to write this book: I found my Company Chicken—and I want to help you find yours, too. Whether it's spot-on chocolate chip cookies (page 182) or a dead simple steak (page 140), forgive yourself for leaning on your go-to's when company comes. In fact, celebrate it. And ask your friends. They just might be hoping you bring out the same ol' cake (or cheesy casserole) when they sit down at your table again.

SWEETS

ALMOST-FAMOUS CRANBERRY BUNDT CAKE

PREP TIME: **25 MINUTES**

TOTAL TIME: **1 HOUR 25 MINUTES**

SERVES **10 TO 12**

This spot-on cake comes from Sarah Kieffer's (wonderful) *Vanilla Bean Baking Book*. I made it a half dozen times within the month the book arrived, so often our whole neighborhood started asking for it. So, maybe it's a stretch to say it's famous, but . . . almost. I tweaked this version with almond flour, less sugar (so we can have it more often), and bitters instead of Grand Marnier, but it's decidedly delicious either way.

As for the glaze, most days I don't think it needs it, but it's definitely seductive when you want to dress this beauty up.

CAKE

1½ cups (3 sticks/336 g) unsalted butter, at room temperature, plus more for the pan

2 cups (400 g) granulated sugar

1 Tbsp grated orange zest

5 large eggs, at room temperature

2 tsp pure vanilla extract

1 hearty dash bitters

2 cups (280 g) all-purpose flour or (310 g) gluten-free flour, plus more for the pan

1 cup (120 g) almond flour

¼ tsp baking soda

¾ tsp fine sea salt

¼ cup (60 ml) fresh squeezed orange juice

1 Tbsp fresh lemon juice

¼ cup (60 ml) half-and-half

2 heaping cups (200 g) cranberries or (280 g) wild blueberries, fresh or frozen

VANILLA-FLECKED GLAZE (OPTIONAL)

1½ cups (180 g) confectioners' sugar

2 to 4 Tbsp half-and-half

Seeds of 1 vanilla bean, scraped, or ¼ tsp vanilla bean paste

Pinch of fine sea salt

cont'd

TO MAKE THE CAKE: Preheat the oven to 350°F (180°C). Position a rack in the lower middle. Butter and flour a 10-inch, 12-cup (25-cm, 2.9-L) nonstick Bundt pan.

Beat together the butter, granulated sugar, and zest in a large bowl with an electric mixer on medium-high speed until light and fluffy, about 2 minutes. Add the eggs one at a time, beating after each until uniform. Scrape down the bottom and sides of the bowl, add the vanilla and bitters, and stir to combine.

In a separate bowl, stir together the flours, baking soda, and salt. Add to the butter mixture in thirds, alternating with the juices and half-and-half, and beat on low to combine, scraping the bowl after each addition. Stir in the cranberries.

Pour the batter into the prepared pan (it will come to the top of the Bundt pan) and bake on a baking sheet until a wooden skewer inserted into the center comes out with a tiny crumb, 1 hour to 1 hour 10 minutes. Transfer to a wire rack to cool for 20 minutes. Remove from the pan, and let cool completely on the rack.

TO MAKE THE GLAZE: Whisk together the confectioners' sugar, half-and-half, vanilla seeds, and salt to make a slightly runny glaze. Set the cake on a wire rack on parchment paper and drizzle the glaze over. Let it set slightly before slicing and serving.

GET AHEAD
This Bundt can be made ahead in two stages: Make the batter, then store in an airtight container in the refrigerator for up to 2 days. Or bake the cake and let cool completely on a metal rack, then freeze, well wrapped, for up to 2 weeks, adding the glaze after thawing it.

GOOD TO KNOW
Be sure to butter and flour your Bundt pan *really* well—those cranberries burst and want to stick if they hit the pan. Use an angel food cake pan for a cleaner, modern look. And get all Jackson Pollock if you want—this is awesome with raspberries, blueberries, or a mix of berries, splattered and streaked ever so slightly.

BITTERS
As the name suggests, bitters are a blend of herbs, barks, roots, and fruits (like orange peel) that lends a pleasantly bitter depth to cocktails and, as in this case, baked goods. If you don't have bitters at home, make your tablespoon of orange zest a heaping one.

If you're a fudgy brownie person, but crave a little more elegance, this is for you. It's deeply rich with cocoa and easy as pie—or, really, much easier. It's not finicky in the way some flourless chocolate cake can be, and you can mask any mistakes (though there's not much to go wrong here) with a dusting of fine cocoa powder or powdered sugar. Dollop with whipped cream or crème fraîche when you serve.

1 cup (2 sticks/225 g) unsalted butter, cut into small pieces, plus more for the pan

¼ cup (60 ml) heavy cream

7 oz (200 g) 70% to 78% bittersweet chocolate, chopped

5 large eggs

1 cup (200 g) sugar

½ cup (40 g) Dutch-processed (or alkalized) cocoa powder, plus more for the pan and garnish

¼ tsp fine sea salt

Lightly sweetened whipped cream (see page 194), or crème fraîche, for serving

Preheat the oven to 350°F (180°C). Butter the bottom and sides of an 8- or 9-inch (20- or 23-cm) spring-form pan and dust it with cocoa powder. Tap out any excess.

Heat the butter and cream in a medium saucepan over low heat. When the butter is melted, add the chopped chocolate and stir frequently until melted and smooth.

In a separate bowl, whisk together the eggs, sugar, cocoa powder, and salt until even and a bit frothy, whisking for 2 to 3 minutes. Stir in the melted chocolate mixture until smooth and even.

cont'd

FLOURLESS CHOCOLATE BROWNIE CAKE

PREP TIME: **30 MINUTES**

TOTAL TIME: **1 HOUR 20 MINUTES**
(includes cooling)

SERVES **8 TO 10**

Transfer the batter to the prepared pan and bake until the cake is puffed and just set through, 35 to 40 minutes. Remove from the oven and let the cake cool for about 40 minutes. Run a knife around the edge and unmold the sides of the springform pan, then transfer the bottom of the pan to a plate or platter (don't try to remove the whole cake from the springform; it may crumble). Sift cocoa powder over the cake before serving. Serve warm or at room temperature with whipped cream.

GET AHEAD

This cake keeps, well wrapped, in the refrigerator for up to 4 days, and freezes fine. You'll lose the distinction of the crackly top layer against the fudgier insides, but it will still be delicious. Bring fully to room temperature before dusting with cocoa or confectioners' sugar and serving with whipped cream or crème fraîche. The whipped cream can be made up to 1 day in advance.

Polenta cakes have an understated loveliness. They are tender, delicately hearty, and such a great canvas for flavor. Mixed with lemon syrup, they hit all the right notes for an afternoon tea or a not-too-sweet after-meal treat. (I get it, lemon bar lovers: There's something special about a tangy curd atop a crumbly crust. But this cake trumps with its texture *and* ease.)

For this simple cake, you can get fancy and sprinkle with rose petals or pistachios. I haven't made that a must here, because I don't want anything to stop you from making this your stalwart weekend superstar that lasts well into the week. The lemon syrup isn't an absolute must either. Whipped cream and berries win here, too.

LEMON-POLENTA SLAB CAKE

PREP TIME: **30 MINUTES**

TOTAL TIME: **1 HOUR 15 MINUTES**

SERVES **16**

CAKE

1¾ cups (3½ sticks/400 g) unsalted butter, at room temperature, plus more for the pan

2 cups (400 g) sugar

Grated zest of 2 lemons (2 Tbsp)

4½ cups (540 g) almond flour

1⅔ cups (230 g) polenta or fine cornmeal

2½ tsp baking powder

¾ tsp fine sea salt

6 large eggs

LEMON DRIZZLE

Juice of 2 lemons (6 Tbsp/90 ml)

⅔ cup (130 g) sugar

TOPPINGS

Warm toasted slivered almonds, rose petals, sesame seeds, shelled Sicilian pistachios (optional)

Preheat the oven to 350°F (180°C). Butter a 9 by 13 inch (23 by 33 cm) baking pan.

TO MAKE THE CAKE: Beat the butter, sugar, and lemon zest in the bowl of a stand mixer fitted with the paddle attachment on medium speed until light and fluffy, scraping down the sides of the bowl occasionally, about 5 minutes.

cont'd

Meanwhile, stir together the almond flour, polenta, baking powder, and salt. Add the eggs to the butter mixture, one at a time, beating well after each addition. Mix in the almond flour mixture on low speed until fully combined, scraping the bottom to be sure all the dry bits are incorporated; the batter will be very thick. Spoon the batter into the prepared pan, smoothing the top with an offset spatula into an even layer. Bake until a cake tester or toothpick comes out mostly clean, 40 to 45 minutes. The cake should have just begun to pull away from the sides of the pan, and be lightly golden brown. Let cool slightly on a wire rack.

WHILE THE CAKE IS STILL HOT, MAKE THE LEMON DRIZZLE:
Simmer the lemon juice and sugar in a small saucepan, stirring occasionally, until the sugar is dissolved. Prick the warm cake all over with a thin cake tester or a toothpick and pour the warm syrup over the top. Let cool before cutting from the pan in 16 neat squares or diamonds. Serve at room temperature.

GET AHEAD
Bake, let cool, and store at room temperature, well wrapped, for up to 4 days.

This is an anytime summer special that's easy to make and wows a crowd with its thick, marbled slabs. It will feel like ice cream, but it's technically a semifreddo (an easier homemade ice cream substitute that slices beautifully)—but no one needs to know that. Slice, serve, and sit back and watch the heads bent over dishes, as your guests silently spoon it in before it melts.

10 chocolate wafer cookies, finely crushed
(about ½ cup/52 g)

2 Tbsp unsalted butter, melted

3 cups (360 g) fresh or frozen raspberries, thawed

1 tsp freshly squeezed lemon juice

1 tsp grated lemon zest

3 large eggs

2 large egg yolks

Seeds of 1 vanilla bean, scraped

1 cup (200 g) sugar

Fine sea salt

1½ cups (360 ml) heavy cream

RASPBERRY RIPPLE ICE CREAM CAKE

PREP TIME: **30 MINUTES**

TOTAL TIME: **6 HOURS**
(includes chill time)

SERVES **6 TO 8**

Line the bottom of an 8½ by 4½ inch (21.5 by 11 cm) loaf pan with waxed paper.

Stir together the cookies and melted butter and set aside. Combine the raspberries, lemon juice, and zest in a high-powered blender and puree until completely smooth. Set aside.

Combine the whole eggs, egg yolks, vanilla bean seeds, sugar, and a pinch of salt in a heatproof bowl, set over a pot of simmering water so that the bowl doesn't touch the water, and cook over medium heat, whisking the eggs constantly, until thick and pale, about 5 minutes. Remove from the heat and beat with an electric mixer until thick and completely cool, 2 to 3 minutes more. Set aside.

In a separate bowl, whip the cream until soft peaks form, 2 to 3 minutes, depending on the speed of your mixer. Gently fold the egg mixture into the whipped cream, taking care to keep it light and airy. (Take a tiny taste at this point; it's so delicious!)

cont'd

Pull out 2 cups (480 ml) of the mixture, put it in a bowl, and fold in the raspberry puree until it is a uniform pink color. Dollop the two mixtures in heaping ladle-fuls, alternating vanilla and raspberry cream, into the prepared pan. You can leave it like this, for a more modern look, or use a skewer or a thin knife to streak and marble the two creams together in places.

Cover tightly with plastic wrap and freeze, level, until it starts to firm up, about 1 hour. When the semifreddo has set a bit (is not jiggly), sprinkle the buttered chocolate cookie crumbs evenly over the top to make a crust, and press them in just slightly. Freeze until completely solid, at least 2 hours and up to 2 days.

To serve the cake, dip an offset spatula into warm water and turn the cake out onto a chilled platter. Slice and serve within 5 minutes; return to the freezer until ready to serve a second round.

GET AHEAD
Because you need it to set up to slice nicely, an icebox cake is just the thing to make far ahead and have at the ready. Make this up to a day in advance, and wrap tightly in plastic wrap, and foil. Because of its lower fat content, freezing it any longer than 2 days can make it turn icy—though still delicious.

Tiramisu is my dad's *and* my husband's favorite dessert—two of the people I love feeding most. But I didn't make it for years, somehow recalling it from culinary school as a laborious task. One night, I decided not to bring home the tempting piece hanging around in the bakery window I passed on my way home from work, and instead make it from scratch. It was a slam dunk. News flash: Unless you're making the lady-fingers yourself—and who is?—tiramisu is easy, and also a built-in make-ahead. You can make this a day ahead, or even two, and still come out looking like an absolute star the day you serve it. Try it for yourself.

EXTRA-ORDINARILY EASY TIRAMISU

PREP TIME: **30 MINUTES**
TOTAL TIME: **2½ HOURS**
(includes chill time)
SERVES **8**

¼ cup (20 g) Dutch-processed (or alkalized) cocoa powder, plus more for dusting

1 cup (240 ml) brewed espresso or strong coffee, piping hot

1 Tbsp pure vanilla extract

5 large egg yolks

½ cup (100 g) sugar

Pinch of fine sea salt

Two 8-oz (226-g) containers mascarpone cheese

1¾ cups (420 ml) heavy cream

24 to 30 ladyfinger cookies

Whisk together the cocoa powder, hot espresso, and vanilla in a bowl until smooth; set aside.

Beat the egg yolks, sugar, and salt in the bowl of a stand mixer fitted with the whisk attachment until pale and thick, about 5 minutes. Beat in the mascarpone until smooth. Add the cream and beat on low speed until the whole mixture feels light and creamy and holds streaks from the beater, about 1 minute.

cont'd

Dunk each ladyfinger, one at a time, in the espresso mixture with a fork, just long enough to absorb the liquid, then arrange half of them in the bottom of a 7 by 11 inch (17 by 28 cm) baking dish. Top with half of the mascarpone mixture, and use a small spatula or a spoon to spread into an even layer. Dust lightly with cocoa powder. Repeat with the remaining ladyfingers and mascarpone. Dust the top lightly with cocoa powder, in an even layer. Cover with plastic wrap and refrigerate until ready to serve, at least 2 hours and up to 2 days. Serve cold.

GET AHEAD

Tiramisu is the perfect make-ahead, as the flavors meld and ladyfingers soften further with time. It will keep, well wrapped, in the refrigerator for up to 2 days.

RAW EGGS?

The signature lightness of this tiramisu comes from raw eggs. We buy them super fresh from the farmers' market, so I never worry, but if raw eggs make you nervous, seek out pasteurized eggs.

There are three kinds of oatmeal cookie: over-sugared and raisin-laden; too *wholesome* (a hippie cookie in disguise); and then these little nuggets of joy you can't stop eating—that *just right* kind of cookie.

These live firmly in the third camp: sugar under control, but present, and no skimping on the butter. Cinnamon and vanilla give these big flavor. And, for the sweet-toothed, a sprinkling of raisins, chocolate chips, and buttery pecans (the ultimate trifecta) do the trick.

1 cup (140 g) all-purpose flour or (155 g) gluten-free flour

½ tsp baking soda

½ tsp baking powder

½ tsp fine sea salt

½ tsp ground cinnamon

½ cup (1 stick/112 g) unsalted butter or coconut oil, melted

¾ cup (145 g) coconut sugar or (150 g) packed dark brown sugar

1 large egg

1 large egg yolk

2 tsp pure vanilla extract

1½ cups (150 g) old-fashioned rolled oats

¾ cup (105 g) plump raisins

¼ to ½ cup (45 to 90 g) chocolate chips or (30 to 60 g) pecans, or a mixture (optional)

PERFECT RATIO OATMEAL-RAISIN COOKIES

PREP TIME: **15 MINUTES**
TOTAL TIME: **30 MINUTES**
MAKES **20 SMALLISH COOKIES**

Preheat the oven to 350°F (180°C). Line two baking sheets with parchment paper or silicone baking mats.

Combine the flour, baking soda, baking powder, salt, and cinnamon in a large bowl. In a separate bowl, whisk together the melted butter, coconut sugar, whole egg, egg yolk, and vanilla, whisking vigorously.

Stir the wet ingredients into the dry ingredients. Stir in the oats, raisins, and chocolate chips and/or pecans, if using, folding into a tight batter. Set the dough aside for 20 minutes while the oven preheats. (This makes them easier to roll into balls, which helps them keep their shape while baking.)

cont'd

Scoop into 20 tablespoon-size balls and roll lightly in barely damp hands to make them round. Spread out on the prepared baking sheets and bake until puffed, golden, and a touch underbaked-looking, 10 to 11 minutes (they will continue to bake on the pans as they cool). Let cool on the pans for 5 minutes before transferring to a wire rack to cool completely.

GOOD TO KNOW
Cookies warm from the oven are always tempting, but wait if you can: the texture of these cookies improves and gets chewier when cooled before eating. I like these best of all a few hours to 1 day after baking, when the brown-sugar flavor settles into every crumb.

DOUGH TO KEEP
This dough keeps super well in the refrigerator for 7 to 10 days, and in the freezer for 1 month (longer and the dough won't spoil, but the flavor loses freshness). But because the butter is melted and there's just enough liquid to hold this dough together, you have to shape them *before* you chill them. See Get Ahead, facing page.

BAKE LIKE A PRO
In case you're asking, *Why melted butter (or coconut oil, if you so choose)?*, there's a reason: Creamed butter produces slightly unpredictable results; if the butter is too soft, cookies weep and spread. Too cold, and the butter doesn't cream well and the finished cookies lack chew. Using melted butter or coconut oil (you won't taste the coconut here) eliminates error. The finished cookies are still moist, but they keep their shape, which makes you look like a pro, even the very first time you make them.

SMART COOKIE GUIDE

SO YOU'RE GLUTEN FREE OR VEGAN? NO SWEAT

No matter your prefernce, here are a few tweaks to make these cookie recipes work for your life.

+ **To make them gluten free:** Use 3 cups (465 g) gluten-free Cup4Cup or Bob's Red Mill Gluten Free 1-to-1 Baking Flour instead of the all-purpose.

+ **To make them vegan:** Replace the butter with coconut oil (melted), and the egg with vegan egg replacer.

+ **To make them nut free:** Use 4 cups (560 g) all-purpose flour or (620 g) gluten-free flour, and skip the almond flour.

+ **To make them sweeter:** Use semisweet chocolate instead of bittersweet.

+ **To make them soft-and-fluffy style:** Add 2 tablespoons cornstarch to the dry ingredients.

GET AHEAD (TWO WAYS)

READY-TO-BAKE ROUNDS: Make the dough and roll into balls. Lay out on a baking sheet and freeze until solid. Store, well wrapped, in plastic containers or zip-top bags, in the refrigerator for 3 days or the freezer for up to 2 weeks.

SLICE-AND-BAKE LOGS: Melted butter makes this dough a good candidate to roll into logs. Put the dough on an 8 by 12 inch (20 by 30.5 cm) sheet of parchment paper. Shape the dough into a log about 1 inch (2.5 cm) from the shorter edge. Wrap in the parchment, using a straight-edged ruler as a guide to pull the dough into a tight log, with the parchment wrapped around it in several layers. Seal the parchment (tuck it or tape it) and refrigerate, well wrapped in plastic and labeled, for up to 2 weeks, or freeze it for up to 1 month. Slice and bake.

Bake the cookies straight from the refrigerator, for about 15 minutes.

If frozen, rest the dough at room temperature for 15 minutes before slicing and baking.

A CHOCOLATE CHIP COOKIE FOR MODERN TIMES

PREP TIME: **15 MINUTES**

TOTAL TIME: **45 MINUTES**

MAKES **ABOUT 36 COOKIES**
(depending on size)

You don't need another fussy chocolate chip cookie recipe. There are plenty out there (confession: I've written my own). What we all need—at least what I, busy working mama of two needed—is an easy, *all-about-the-chocolate* chocolate chip cookie recipe to turn to again and again—something akin to the Toll House of my youth, but even quicker, way more beautiful, and reliably irresistible.

That's how years after thinking I would never tackle the most beloved cookie of all time again, I did. The result, below, is the recipe I now lean on again and again when we're short on time but craving something as close as possible to spooning warm melted chocolate directly into our mouths, without actually doing it.

This cookie is easy in that dump-and-stir way, thanks to the melted butter (no softening butter, no beating); and is not a sugar bomb, thanks to almond flour and *just right* ratios of sugar and chocolate. The result is a chewy cookie with a deep toffee-like flavor, and generous bursts of warm chocolate—an improved-upon version of the warm chocolate chip cookie of my childhood, for modern times.

3 cups (420 g) all-purpose flour

1 cup (120 g) almond flour

1½ cups (300 g) light brown sugar or (290 g) coconut sugar

½ cup (100 g) granulated sugar

1½ tsp baking soda

1 tsp flaky sea salt, such as Maldon, plus more for sprinkling

1 cup (2 sticks/225 g) unsalted butter, melted

2 large eggs, at room temperature

2 tsp pure vanilla extract

15 oz (470 g) bittersweet chocolate, chopped

Preheat the oven to 375°F (190°C). Line two baking sheets with parchment paper or silicone baking mats.

cont'd

Whisk together the flours, sugars, baking soda, and salt in a medium bowl. In a separate small bowl, whisk together the melted butter, eggs, and vanilla, whisking vigorously. Stir the wet ingredients into the dry ingredients. Mix in the chocolate, reserving just a bit for the tops, making sure they're evenly distributed throughout the dough.

Scoop the dough by heaping tablespoons and roll into balls between your hands. Arrange on the prepared baking sheets with plenty of space between them. Press reserved chocolate into the tops of the cookies. Bake, one sheet at a time, until crispy on the outside edges and soft and just a touch underbaked-looking inside (they will continue to bake on the pan as they cool), 10 to 12 minutes.

Remove from the oven and sprinkle with salt—or skip it if that's not your thing. Let cool on the pan for at least 2 minutes (they may fall apart if you pull them off too hot), before transferring to plates to serve warm, when they're best.

GET AHEAD

This is my big-batch recipe. Because the dough only improves with time, it's worth hanging on to some. We bake a dozen right away, then save the rest for sheet-by-sheet baking as needed. If you bake two sheets at a time, rotate the trays and switch them from the top to bottom rack halfway through baking for even browning.

In a nutshell, my childhood summers were Big Wheels and mosquito bites, white-trimmed shorts riding high above skinned knees, and tender, marshmallow-studded rhubarb cake. My mom's beloved cake is hard to top—but the essence of childhood is truly present in this stripped-down summer dessert: tender and tart, crumbly and just a tiny touch sweet. Don't skip the generous scoops of ice cream right on top. Check all formalities for the night: pass the spoons and dig straight in.

TOPPING

1 cup (140 g) all-purpose flour or (155 g) gluten-free flour

1 cup (100 g) rolled oats

⅓ cup (65 g) sugar, plus more for sprinkling

½ tsp fine sea salt

½ cup (1 stick/112 g) unsalted butter, melted

¼ cup (about 30 g) walnuts, almonds, sunflower seeds, or a mixture, roughly chopped

FILLING

5 stalks rhubarb, sliced (about 4 cups/350 g)

3 cups (360 g) raspberries

⅓ cup (65 g) sugar

3 Tbsp cornstarch

Ice cream, for serving

Cold cream or half-and-half, for serving

Preheat the oven to 375°F (190°C).

TO MAKE THE TOPPING: Combine the flour, oats, sugar, and salt in a bowl and stir together. Toss the melted butter into the flour, creating a mixture that resembles coarse bread crumbs. Add half of the nuts and pinch together to make a tight dough.

cont'd

RASPBERRY-RHUBARB CRUMBLE

PREP TIME: **15 MINUTES**

TOTAL TIME: **1 HOUR 20 MINUTES**

SERVES **6**

TO MAKE THE FILLING: Combine the rhubarb, raspberries, sugar, and cornstarch in a bowl and toss to combine. Transfer to a 2-qt (2-L) round or oval casserole dish or deep-dish pie plate. Top with the crumble topping, letting a bit of the fruit peek out the sides. Sprinkle with the remaining nuts and bake until golden and bubbling, 30 to 40 minutes. Serve warm, with ice cream scooped right onto the top, a drizzle of fresh cold cream, and a stack of spoons.

GET AHEAD
You can assemble this dessert and wrap, unbaked, in the refrigerator, up to overnight. To prep further ahead: The topping can be made into clumps, and refrigerated or frozen for up to 1 week. Make the filling, assemble, and bake as instructed.

GOOD TO KNOW
This is a smallish cobbler, to be eaten from the dish with an intimate group, but it doubles well for a crowd. Bake it in a 9 by 13 inch (23 by 33 cm) pan.

EASIER-THAN-PIE WARM APPLE TART (IT'S TRUE)

PREP TIME: **15 MINUTES**

TOTAL TIME: **1 HOUR**

SERVES **6**

This tart came to be one Sunday when all I could think about was baking a pie. But there's never time for baking a pie, even on the weekend, at least not between planting blackberries and visiting with friends and long bouts of begging a toddler to take a nap. But there is time, almost any day, to make this.

The idea came from my friend Aran Goyoaga, of *Cannelle et Vanille*, who is always arranging fruit in tarts in such elegant ways. The filling has all the goods of apple pie with a quarter of the work, tucked into a press-in crust so easy my seven-year-old can make it on her own.

This tart is hard to cut warm, but it melts in your mouth (and no one minds a warm crumbled apple tart spooned into a bowl, with ice cream melting on top). Cool, it is equally alluring and easier to serve in perfect slices. The best thing about this tart, though, besides eating it, is knowing how easy it is to make it again.

¾ cup (1½ sticks/178 g) unsalted butter, melted, plus ¼ cup (½ stick/56 g), cut into cubes

¾ cup (90 g) almond flour

¾ cup (117 g) gluten-free flour or (105 g) all-purpose flour

⅓ cup (65 g) sugar

1 tsp pure vanilla extract

Pinch of sea salt

Pinch of freshly ground black pepper (optional)

4 crisp, tart apples, such as Ginger Gold or Jonathan (about 1½ lb/680 g)

¼ tsp ground cinnamon

1 tsp fresh lemon juice

TOPPINGS

Pistachios, fresh herbs, or rose petals (optional)

Whipped cream or ice cream

Stir together the melted butter, almond flour, gluten-free flour, 2 tablespoons of the sugar, the vanilla, salt, and pepper (if using) in a bowl to make a sandy paste. Press into the bottom and up the sides of a

cont'd

9-inch (23-cm) tart pan with a removable bottom (a 9-inch/23-cm springform pan will work, if that's all you have). Chill in the freezer while you preheat the oven, 20 to 30 minutes.

Preheat the oven to 400°F (200°C). Position a rack in the middle of the oven.

Cut the cheeks of the apples off the core into four pieces (each piece will have one large flat side). Lay them on their flat sides and thinly slice each piece, holding them together in their shape as you go. Arrange the slices around the tart in any pattern you desire, fanning the apples just a bit; use them all, even if you have to squeeze some of the slices in. (Don't overthink it; it doesn't have to be perfect!) Sprinkle evenly with the remaining sugar and the cinnamon, and dot with the cubed butter.

Bake until the crust is toasty and golden and the apples are tender, 35 to 40 minutes. Sprinkle with the lemon juice and any additional garnishes you desire. Serve with whipped cream.

GET AHEAD
The crust keeps, unbaked and well wrapped, in the freezer for up to 3 weeks. After serving your gorgeous tart, and before you store away your clean tart pan, make and press in another crust. Wrap well in plastic film and freeze to have on hand as a head start for surprise company.

GOOD TO KNOW
I always use firm, tart local apples with beautiful skins for this tart—either red or golden-yellow. You can adjust the amount of lemon you include to how tart your apples are—starting with 1 teaspoon. Don't use Granny Smith apples for this; the skin is too tough.

GLUTEN FREE, OR NOT
I most often use almond flour and gluten-free flour for this crust, so it's both tender and nutty, and completely gluten free—a win for parties and mixed crowds. This works beautifully with all-purpose flour, too, if that's what you have and use at home.

András's mother raised two big-appetite boys (five if you include her grandsons). Part of her winning formula was a weekly batch of baked rice pudding. It is ripe with all the substantive vanilla custard satisfaction that only a rice pudding can offer, and it's super-smart for feeding a crowd. From a single pan, there's enough for warm dessert one night, a filling on-the-go breakfast square for the next day, and a late-day snack later in the week. And really, what could be better than that?

2 cups (400 g) white rice, rinsed and drained

8 cups (2 L) whole milk

1⅓ cups (265 g) sugar

Pinch of fine sea salt

1 vanilla bean, seeds scraped

8 large eggs, separated

Grated zest of 1 lemon

HUNGARIAN BAKED RICE PUDDING

PREP TIME: **25 MINUTES**

TOTAL TIME: **2 HOURS**
(includes cooling)

SERVES **8 TO 12** with leftovers

Preheat the oven to 350°F (180°C). Generously butter a 9 by 13 inch (23 by 33 cm) baking pan.

Combine the rice, milk, half of the sugar, the salt, and vanilla bean seeds in a saucepan. Bring to a boil, then lower the heat and simmer, stirring occasionally, uncovered, until the rice is tender, 15 to 20 minutes. Set aside to cool completely.

Combine the egg yolks, lemon zest, and the remaining sugar in a bowl, and whisk vigorously until lightened. Spoon into the rice mixture and stir to combine.

Beat the egg whites with an electric mixer until stiff and glossy, about 4 minutes. Fold into the pudding until evenly combined. Transfer the pudding to the prepared baking pan and bake until puffy and golden brown, 45 to 55 minutes. Let cool completely, then cover and refrigerate until ready to serve. Cut the rice pudding into 15 squares and serve at room temperature, or refrigerate for up to 3 days.

GET AHEAD
Bake the pudding all the way
through, let cool completely, then
wrap tightly and refrigerate for up
to 3 days. Don't freeze; the rice and
custard separate after defrosting.

SO YOU WHIPPED SOME CREAM. NOW WHAT?

If you are not whipping your own cream, you're missing out. Perfect, dollopable cream is an art form worth mastering. To do it: Whip 1 cup (240 ml) of the best, freshest heavy cream you can find in a metal bowl with a whisk or electric beater until it just holds its shape. Fold in 1 teaspoon sugar and a splash of pure vanilla extract. Test with a spoon—it should slide right off but still hold some shape. Use a whisk to finish it off, whipping a few times by hand until it just holds soft peaks—but no further: It should dollop lusciously over any cake or pie. Makes 2 cups (240 g) whipped cream.

Here are three no-fuss but still fantastic desserts to make with it, in minutes.

ETON MESS: Mash 1 cup (120 g) ripe berries with ¼ cup (50 g) sugar and set aside for 10 minutes. Fold the berries and their juices into 2 cups (240 g) soft whipped cream. Serve cold, or sprinkle with crushed meringue and serve in cups. Serves 6.

FAUX LEMON-MAPLE MOUSSE: Whip 1 cup (240 ml) heavy cream with 1 tablespoon grated lemon zest (to make 2 cups [240 g] whipped cream). Combine 2 tablespoons maple syrup with 1 to 2 tablespoons fresh lemon juice, and fold into the cream. Chill until ready to serve, or at least 1 hour. Serves 6.

CHOCOLATE MASCARPONE CAKE: Combine 1¾ cups (175 g) crushed chocolate wafer cookies with 6 tablespoons (¾ stick/84 g) melted unsalted butter. Press into the bottom of a 9-inch (23-cm) tart pan with a removable bottom. Fold ½ cup (115 g) mascarpone cheese (at room temperature) and ¼ cup (50 g) sugar into 1 heaping cup (120 g) soft whipped cream; stir to combine. Spoon into the tart shell. Bring ½ cup (120 ml) heavy cream to a simmer and pour it over 4 ounces (120 g) chopped bittersweet or semisweet chocolate and whisk until completely smooth; let cool. Pour over the mascarpone layer and smooth with an offset spatula. Chill until firm, 2 hours or up to overnight. Garnish with berries or fresh currants. Serves 10.

DRINKS & TONICS

My family drinks this juice many days of the week, not because we're super health nuts, but because I know I can count on it to get in our greens, which takes the pressure off the rest of the day. Plus, this is so delicious, everyone asks for seconds, even my three-year-old.

This is *green* juice: emphasis on the green, not on the juice (read: not that sweet). Younger, smaller kale and celery leaves yield a slightly sweeter result; bigger mature leaves will be more intense. If you're new to green juice, or if you know you prefer a sweet*ish* beverage that is *just* green enough, use a whole banana and coconut water instead of plain water.

2 handfuls (1 oz/30 g) baby kale or chopped kale, ribs removed

½ to 1 whole banana (your preference)

1 stalk young celery

1 tart, juicy apple, cut into pieces

2 Tbsp fresh lemon juice

One 1-inch (2.5-cm) piece fresh ginger, peeled (optional)

1 cup (240 ml) water or coconut water

1 handful ice cubes (about 1 cup/150 g)

Blend the kale, banana, celery, apple, lemon juice, ginger (if using), water, and ice in a powerful blender until completely smooth and frothy; pour into a chilled glass and enjoy.

EVERYDAY GREEN JUICE

SERVES **2**
(makes about 2½ cups/600 ml)

GOOD TO KNOW

When possible, I use only organic fruits and vegetables for juicing, for the highest quality drink. For a milder kale taste, use baby kale, or remove the spine down the back of more mature kale before blending.

We are big milkshake fans. Double thick. But this baby tricks us into thinking we don't need ice cream at all. Think of this as a shake, light: a frothy, cool, cocoa-y fix that works for snack, sweet, or even breakfast (in that case, add protein powder for oomph).

1 large banana

⅓ cup (25 g) cocoa powder

1 tsp raw coconut oil

1 Tbsp raw honey

1¼ cups (300 ml) whole milk, almond milk, or almond-coconut milk blend

Pinch of fine sea salt

Pinch of ground cinnamon

1 handful ice cubes (about 1 cup/150 g)

Blend everything except the ice in a powerful blender until completely smooth. When everything is smooth and even, add the ice and blend until frothy. Pour into a chilled glass and enjoy.

RAW COCOA-HONEY ANYTIME SHAKE

SERVES **2**
(makes about 3 cups/720 ml)

GOOD TO KNOW

If you like something thicker and sweeter, add an extra banana or 4 pitted dates to the blender before you add the other ingredients, and blend until completely smooth.

Sometimes late at night I crave a little something creamy. This simple, sweet concoction always does the trick. It's the cold answer to the warm milk and honey my children sometimes ask for before bed. The orange flower water is a nod to a flavor I fell in love with from North Africa via France and tastes just right here. Go easy, especially if you haven't used it before; you can bump it up a bit after you fall in love.

½ cup (120 ml) cold heavy cream

½ cup (120 ml) cold water

2 Tbsp honey

2 cups (480 g) cold plain yogurt

2 ice cubes

1 tsp orange flower water (optional)

Saffron, for garnish (optional)

Put two glasses in the freezer to chill. Whip the cream to soft peaks and return to the refrigerator to chill.

Combine the water, honey, yogurt, ice, and orange flower water (if using) in a blender, and blend until light and frothy, covered with bubbles over the top. Spoon a bit of whipped cream into the bottom of each of the chilled glasses. Pour the lassi over the cream and top with saffron threads, if desired. Serve chilled.

FROTHED SAFFRON LASSI

SERVES **2**
(makes about 2½ cups/600 ml)

GET AHEAD
The cream can be whipped up to several hours in advance and combined in a glass with the other ingredients just before serving.

GOOD TO KNOW
The saffron here is mostly for color and garnish; it's an expensive ingredient, so if it's not something you already keep on hand, skip it.

RASPBERRY SHRUB

SERVES **10**
(makes 2 cups/480 ml)

A shrub is a simple fermented drink, made with slightly off berries doused in vinegar and sugar—sometimes called drinking vinegar. That's not a good advertisement, but it deserves saying it up front because this tangy beverage may take some adjusting to. Once you get used to it, wow, it is refreshing. Think of a shrub as a cheater's kombucha—faster and simpler to make. It is the perfect 3 p.m. *almost* sweet fizzy drink to perk me up when I'm pushing through to the end of the workday.

2 cups (240 g) fresh raspberries

1 cup (200 g) unbleached sugar

Peel of 1 lemon

¼ cup (3 g) fresh mint leaves

1 cup (240 ml) apple cider vinegar

Sparkling water or seltzer, for serving

Combine the raspberries, sugar, lemon peel, and mint in a jar and muddle a bit, pressing out some of the juice. Cover tightly and refrigerate for 1 day.

Remove from the refrigerator, muddle slightly with a wooden spoon or potato masher, and add the vinegar. Stir to dissolve any remaining sugar. Some people strain it at this point, but I don't (I love the bits of raspberry). Keep in the refrigerator for 3 to 6 days.

To serve, shake the shrub, spoon about 2 tablespoons into a glass, and top with sparkling water or seltzer (about ½ cup/120 ml, give or take). Serve cold.

There's a Oaxacan restaurant midway between my son's nursery school and our home, where we stop for a bite once a week. Sometimes we get flautas and tamales, but mostly we belly up to the bar and spend the first five minutes trying to remember if it's the watermelon or the pineapple agua fresca we all love so much. After we order a round of both, everyone ends up fighting over last sips of the frothy pineapple drink.

"There's no sugar in this, right?" I asked the host one day, after we'd been there about a dozen times. "Just a touch," she said with a wink. Make it without, as I often do, but just that teaspoon or two brings this to the next level: our off-season drinkable ice pop.

½ **very ripe pineapple**

1 to 2 tsp sugar (optional)

About ½ cup (75 g) ice cubes

1 cup (240 ml) water

Juice of ½ lime (about 2 tsp)

Trim the pineapple: peel and core it (and save the fibrous core for smoothies). Chop the remainder—you should have about 3 cups (420 g). Put in a powerful blender with the sugar and pulse to chop. Add enough ice and water to fill the blender to the top, about 1½ cups (360 ml) total, and add the lime juice. Blend until completely smooth and frothy. (Some people strain at this point, but I don't bother—give me all the pulp and all the flavor.) Pour over fresh ice or into a chilled glass and enjoy.

PINEAPPLE AGUA FRESCA

SERVES **2 TO 4**
(makes about 4 cups/960 ml)

GOOD TO KNOW

This is a great punch to serve with the taco feast for a crowd (page 146). Use a whole trimmed pineapple and double the recipe (blending it in batches) to serve 4 to 8.

Pictured: 1 Raw Cocoa-Honey Anytime Shake 2 Raspberry Shrub
3 Pineapple Agua Fresca 4 Frothed Saffron Lassi 5 Cucumber
Cooler 6 Everyday Green Juice 7 Strawberry-Watermelon Smoothie

This is for those who crave that clean cucumber flavor that nothing else can replace. Start with young, garden-fresh or thin-skinned cucumbers (big, thick-skinned cucumbers can be bitter), and drink right after blending.

1 small fresh cucumber (10 oz/300 g), sliced, plus more for garnish

¼ cup (60 ml) fresh grapefruit juice

1 handful ice cubes (about 1 cup/150 g)

One 1-inch (2.5-cm) piece of ginger, peeled

1 tsp sugar

1 cup (240 ml) sparkling water or ginger ale

Blend the cucumber, ice, grapefruit juice, ginger, and sugar in a powerful blender until smooth. Pour into a chilled glass, top with sparkling water, and garnish with cucumber. Enjoy.

CUCUMBER COOLER

SERVES **2**
(makes 2 cups/480 ml)

GOOD TO KNOW
You can play with the flavor here by adding jalapeño, ginger, lime juice, or basil to the blender with the cucumber.

This is summer in a glass, so simple, and refreshing enough to serve on a sweltering afternoon, but welcome at breakfast time, too. (It's also a perfect starter for a margarita crowd.)

½ baby watermelon (about 1½ lb/720 g), peeled and cubed (about 3 cups/450 g)

1 cup (120 g) fresh or frozen strawberries

1 handful ice cubes (about 1 cup/150 g)

3 Tbsp fresh lime juice

½ cup (120 ml) coconut milk

1 Tbsp honey (optional)

Blend the watermelon, strawberries, ice, lime juice, coconut milk, and honey (if using) in a powerful blender until completely smooth and frothy, pour over ice or into a chilled glass, and enjoy.

STRAWBERRY-WATERMELON SMOOTHIE

SERVES **2 TO 4**
(makes about 4 cups/960 ml)

INFINITELY REPEATABLE SMOOTHIES

EACH SERVES **2**
(makes 1½ to 2 cups/360 to 480 ml each)

Most mornings, still shuffling in slippers, my kids and I raid the refrigerator for supplies, climb on the counter (the kids, not me), and blend up a smoothie or juice. Most are a cross between juice and smoothie, and many are green, to get those greens in the system first thing. But sometimes we're feeling tropical (pineapple!) or hankering for something rich and filling (peanut butter!).

There are not a lot of ways to mess up a smoothie; most days I get a *This is a good one!* from my crowd—and I'm hoping you do, too. Here are our five favorite formulas. Play around and get creative. My rule of thumb: Less is more. Use more than five or six ingredients, and everything tastes a little murky. Stick to basics and don't forget that smoothies aren't shakes: Go easy on the sweet stuff.

For each smoothie, blend all the ingredients in a blender until frothy and smooth; serve right away.

MANGO TURMERIC MORNING CRUSH

½ frozen banana

1 cup (165 g) fresh or frozen mango chunks

1 cup (240 ml) coconut milk (from the can) or kefir

One ½-inch (12-mm) piece fresh ginger, peeled

1 tsp ground turmeric

Pinch of ground cinnamon (optional)

1 tsp honey or maple syrup (or to taste)

BANANAS GOOD

1 banana

½ cup (70 g) raw cashews

1 cup (240 ml) Homemade Oat-Almond Milk (page 219) or unsweetened almond milk

2 to 3 pitted Medjool dates

¼ tsp ground cinnamon

½ tsp pure vanilla extract

1 handful ice (about 1 cup/150 g)

GET UP AND GREEN SHAKE

1 frozen banana

1 packed cup (20 g) greens (baby spinach, stemmed kale, collards, chard, etc.)

1 cup (140 g) chopped pineapple

1 cup (240 ml) unsweetened kefir or plain yogurt

EVERYONE'S FAVORITE BERRY SHAKE

½ frozen banana

1 cup (120 g) frozen raspberries or strawberries

1 cup (240 ml) whole milk, Homemade Oat-Almond Milk (page 219), or unsweetened almond milk

½ cup (120 g) plain yogurt

Splash of pure vanilla extract

1 tsp honey or maple syrup (or to taste)

THE NUTTER BUTTER SHAKE

1 cup (240 g) plain yogurt

4 pitted Medjool dates

¼ cup (60 g) peanut or almond butter

½ cup (120 ml) whole milk, Homemade Oat-Almond Milk (page 219), or unsweetened almond milk

½ cup (75 g) ice

I am not Italian, not by a long stretch. But legends of Sunday gatherings around a big pot of Nonna's sauce or gravy (a thick, meat-laden tomato sauce that cooks all day, to be spooned over pasta and sopped up with chewy bread) made me wish that I was.

Sunday sauce is a force, the kind of cooking that fills the house with aromas and people—the kind of cooking I want happening in my home. It is also just about the best way to prepare for the week ahead.

You do not have to be Italian to adopt this tradition as your own. A pot of this simmering sauce is the most satisfying thing to come home to on a cool fall day, or stay home and fuss over on a blustery winter one. I decided to stop fantasizing about it and start making it week by week, because spooning up portions of this over tubetti, linguine, or spaghetti makes me feel like a proper mama, the kind with a revolving door of guests at the table because yours is the best Sunday sauce on the block.

SUNDAY SAUCE

PREP TIME: **25 MINUTES**

TOTAL TIME: **2½ HOURS**

SERVES **6 TO 8**
(makes 8 cups/2 L)

2 Tbsp olive oil

1 lb (455 g) beef short ribs, English (or flanken) style

1 tsp fine sea salt, plus more for seasoning the sauce

1½ lb (680 g) Italian sausages, sweet or mild

4 garlic cloves, peeled

¼ cup (60 g) tomato paste

Two 28-oz (794-g) cans whole peeled San Marzano tomatoes

2 tsp soy sauce (optional; see Good to Know, page 214)

6 fresh basil leaves, torn

1 batch sopressata meatballs (page 109; optional)

1 lb (455 g) rigatoni, spaghetti, linguine, or shells, cooked

Grated Parmesan or pecorino romano cheese

Bitter Greens and Beets Salad (page 144)

Italian bread, for serving

Heat the oil in a large heavy pot over medium heat. Pat the ribs dry, season on all sides with salt, and add to the hot oil. Cook, turning occasionally, until the

cont'd

pieces are browned on all sides, about 15 minutes. Transfer to a plate. Add the sausages and brown on all sides. Set aside with the ribs. Drain any excess fat from the pot, reserving about 2 tablespoons.

Add the garlic to the pot and cook until fragrant and golden brown, about 2 minutes. Discard the garlic, then stir the tomato paste into the fat in the pot. Cook for about 1 minute, then add the tomatoes, crushing them well between your fingers or with a potato masher. Add 1½ to 2 cups (360 to 480 ml) water, the ribs, sausages, soy sauce (if using), and basil, and bring to a simmer. Cover the pot loosely and cook over medium-low heat, stirring every 30 minutes or so, until the sauce is slightly thickened, about 2 hours.

While the sauce cooks, brown the meatballs (if using), in a little fat in a separate pan, turning to cook on all sides, about 2 minutes per side (don't cook them through—they'll finish in the sauce).

When the sauce is deeply flavorful, add the meatballs and cook until the sauce is thick and the meats are all very tender, 30 minutes more.

Meanwhile, cook the pasta in salted boiling water; drain, reserving a bit of the pasta-cooking water.

Pull the meat and some of the sauce out of the pot and arrange on a platter. Toss the remaining sauce with the pasta, and serve alongside the meat, with tons of freshly shaved Parmesan over the top. Serve with the salad and, of course, Italian bread. Refrigerate in an airtight container for up to 5 days.

GOOD TO KNOW
I like to use English, flanken, or Korean-cut short ribs in my sauce, but oxtail or osso bucco would also work great here. One day I threw some leftover soy-braised short ribs (page 106) into my Sunday gravy, and they were the best batch yet. That's how a splash of soy became part of my formula.

My last few years in New York City, we lived in Astoria, where Greek restaurants line every block. Every morning I walked cross-town to take Greta to school, then rode the subway the opposite way for work. Spinach pie was never on my radar, but on many a cold winter morning, I'd pass a tiny deli right near the subway with the smell of strong coffee and hot, freshly made spinach pie spilling into the street. Often, that hot spinach pie, eaten straight from the foil wrapping, warmed more than just my bones. It was a link to something bigger.

On nicer days, I'd tuck it into my purse and find the same pie, cooled, more chewy and slightly more spinach-forward, just as satisfying eaten hours later at my desk.

Spinach pie is easily made at home; don't let the unknown (phyllo dough) hold you back. Sure, it cracks and rips a bit, but that won't hurt anything. This addictive pie is invitingly hot and crispy on the countertop on a spring weekend or, that surprising little gift, cold but delicious from your fridge for a quick deskside lunch. It tastes great with a warm soup or alone with a glass of wine. And just when you least expect it, it might even save the day.

SAVE-THE-DAY SPINACH PIE

PREP TIME: 25 MINUTES
TOTAL TIME: 1½ HOURS
SERVES **8**

30 oz (860 g) frozen spinach, thawed

½ cup (1 stick/112 g) unsalted butter

1 small yellow onion, finely chopped

2 cups (480 g) whole-milk ricotta cheese

4 large eggs, lightly beaten

⅓ cup (40 g) crumbled feta cheese

3 Tbsp chopped fresh dill (optional)

Juice of 1 lemon

1 tsp fine sea salt

¼ tsp freshly ground black pepper

8 sheets frozen phyllo dough, thawed

Preheat the oven to 375°F (190°C).

cont'd

Set the spinach in a colander to drain while you prepare the remaining ingredients, then place it in the center of a large, sturdy dish towel. Squeeze out as much moisture as you can. (If you wash the towel shortly after, the color won't stain.)

Heat a large pan over medium heat. Melt the butter, and pour off and reserve about 5 tablespoons. Add the onion to the skillet and cook until soft but not brown, about 5 minutes. Transfer to a bowl with the squeezed spinach, and add the ricotta, eggs, feta, dill (if using), lemon juice, salt, and pepper.

Brush a 9 by 11 inch (23 by 33 cm) baking pan with some of the reserved melted butter. Lay the two first sheets of phyllo side by side in the bottom of the pan to cover it and come 1 inch (2.5 cm) up the sides; brush with butter. Continue with another two sheets of phyllo right on top, layering them slightly overlapping to cover the bottom and up the sides (so far, you've used four sheets). Add the spinach mixture and spread into an even layer. Lay two more sheets of phyllo side by side on top, to cover the entire filling, and brush with butter. Tuck the sides of the phyllo over the top, and layer the two remaining sheets of phyllo on top. Brush with the remaining butter.

Bake until the phyllo is cooked through, shiny, and golden brown, 40 to 45 minutes. Remove and let cool until just warm to the touch before cutting. Cut into 9 or 12 pieces and serve warm or at room temperature. Refrigerate any leftovers in an airtight container for up to 3 days.

DOUBLE UP

One pan is a great start, but two pans of spinach pie will have you set for one hot meal, plus packable lunches and late-day snacks. Cool one pan completely and freeze, well wrapped (in plastic wrap *and* foil, right in the pan), for up to 2 weeks. To eat, bring to room temperature first, then warm in a hot oven for 5 minutes.

EASY CHICKEN LIVER PÂTÉ

PREP TIME: **5 MINUTES**

TOTAL TIME: **30 MINUTES**

SERVES **6**
(makes 1 cup/240 ml)

I know what you're thinking: Why would a pâté recipe belong in a book that promises easy cooking? Hear me out. Making a little pot of chicken liver pâté is *easy*—far easier than trying to hunt down a good pre-pared pâté if you don't live in a big city! Plus, if you're buying whole chickens, chances are you're getting a few chicken livers each time. (Save them up in a con-tainer in the freezer until you have about 1 cup/about 240 g.) It only takes a simple sauté with some shallots and butter, and a blender, to whip up this little pot of luxury that's an easy make-ahead wow for any of the Grazing Platters on pages 92 to 100.

½ cup (1 stick/112 g) unsalted butter, cut into pieces

1 shallot, thinly sliced

1 cup (about 240 g) fresh chicken livers, trimmed

⅓ cup (80 ml) spiced pear liqueur, port, or Madeira

¼ cup (60 ml) heavy cream

Flaky sea salt, such as Maldon

Freshly ground black pepper

Crackers and toast, for serving

Heat half of the butter in a large pan over medium heat. When it foams, add the shallot and cook until soft, but without any color or browning. Add the livers and the liqueur, and increase the heat to high. Cook, stirring the livers with a spoon, until the livers are lightly brown but still soft and pink inside, and the liqueur has reduced, about 5 minutes.

Remove from the heat, transfer to a blender along with the cream and remaining butter, and blend until smooth. Taste and add salt and pepper as necessary, adding more cream if desired (the pâté will set up and get thicker as it rests in the refrigerator).

Pack the pâté into a small pot or jar, and smooth the top with a spatula. Cover with plastic wrap and refrigerate until firm, about 2 hours, or up to 3 days. Serve with crackers and toast.

For many things, commercial nut milks do the trick (look for ones made with more nuts and less gums and fillers). I use them for baking. But homemade nut milks are a whole other story: Blending almonds with oats makes a thick and creamy milk that I love. The oats give a round familiarity and a richness that makes this a treat to drink straight, add to smoothies, or whip into a latte. As a ritual, I stir in cinnamon and honey, and keep it in big jars in the refrigerator every week, where a quick shake and pour yields a delicious, horchata-like milk drink that I feel good about drinking day after day.

2 cups (280 g) whole raw almonds

½ cup (50 g) rolled or quick-cooking oats

¼ tsp fine sea salt

¼ tsp ground cinnamon

½ tsp pure vanilla extract

2 Tbsp honey, or to taste (optional)

Soak the almonds, oats, salt, and cinnamon in 8 cups (2 L) water on the countertop for 3 hours, or better yet, overnight. Puree in a blender on high speed until completely smooth, about 3 minutes. Strain through a medium-mesh strainer and press the pulp, getting out as much creamy milk as you can without going crazy (this extra step takes about 5 minutes).

Pour into a clean glass jar or bottle, seal, and refrigerate for up to 5 days. To use, shake well before pouring. Stir in vanilla and honey (if desired), and serve cold.

HOMEMADE OAT-ALMOND MILK

PREP TIME: **5 MINUTES**

TOTAL TIME: **4 TO 12 HOURS**
(includes soaking)

MAKES **6½ CUPS (1.5 L)**

THE ONLY GREEN SAUCE YOU NEED

PREP TIME: **5 MINUTES**

TOTAL TIME: **10 MINUTES**

MAKES ¾ **CUP/ 5 OZ/ 130 G**

At any time, I have a green sauce working for me (read: at the ready to spoon or swoosh onto every plate). It has the power to make any otherwise unmemorable meal come to life. It might be made with a bag of prewashed kale, leftover herb bits, or wild mustard gathered from the yard; it doesn't matter. What does matter is that *green sauce* (no other name needed) is a one-size-fits-all accessory you can count on, with oodles of flexibility and a very forgiving tone. You can add nuts (à la pesto—be they almonds, pepitas, or pine nuts), or make it straight up with greens and a glug of your best olive oil.

I store mine on the top shelf of my refrigerator in a glass container, where I can see it, use it, and replenish it with ease all week long.

1 bunch fresh parsley, cilantro, arugula, mustard greens, or another punchy green (about 3 packed cups)

1 small bunch fresh chives

Juice of 1 lemon or lime (about 2 Tbsp)

1 small garlic clove, peeled

2 to 4 Tbsp olive oil

¼ cup something with body (¼ avocado, nuts, miso, tahini, etc.)

¾ tsp sea salt (give or take)

½ tsp freshly ground black pepper (give or take)

Add the greens, chives, lemon juice, garlic, olive oil, avocado, sea salt, and pepper in a blender and pulse until broken down and easy to dollop with a spoon (adding a tablespoon of water if needed to thin and get the blender going).

SMEAR ON: Toast, veggies, cheese sandwiches.

DRIZZLE OVER: Grilled fish, fried eggs, savory yogurt bowls, roasted vegetables.

GET AHEAD

Transfer to a container that just fits and top with a little more oil (to preserve color); keep in the refrigerator for up to 1 week.

EVERYDAY DRESSINGS

Making one of these dressings isn't a project: Each takes about 5 minutes. But while you have the blender out, make all three and tuck them away to reap the rewards at every meal.

LEMON–SHALLOT VINAIGRETTE

MAKES **1 CUP (240 ml)** and doubles easily

This classic deserves to be in every refrigerator in the country as a reliably bracing and just-rich-enough coating for a bed of any greens or vegetables.

1 small shallot, minced
¾ cup (180 ml) extra-virgin olive oil
¼ cup (60 ml) fresh lemon juice
2 tsp Dijon mustard
1 tsp honey
½ tsp fine sea salt, or to taste
½ tsp freshly ground black pepper, or to taste

Puree all the ingredients in a blender until smooth, seasoning with salt and pepper to taste. Serve, or refrigerate in an airtight container for up to 8 days.

USE WITH: The Ravenwood Salad (page 134).

ALSO GREAT WITH: Any greens, fish, roasted vegetables (for dipping).

TAHINI GREEN GODDESS DRESSING

MAKES 3½ **CUPS (840 ML)**

Tahini works to add a salty, creamy finish to dips and dressings, like this one, which is punchy from loads of parsley. Here, it works to deepen the delight of this age-old dressing. Keep this heavy hitter on hand; it has many allies (see suggestions, below).

2 garlic cloves, smashed

1½ cups (360 g) plain whole-milk yogurt

1 cup (240 g) tahini

⅓ cup (80 ml) fresh lemon juice

1½ cups (20 g) packed fresh parsley leaves

2 tsp fine sea salt

1 tsp freshly ground black pepper

Puree all the ingredients and 2 tablespoons water in a blender until smooth and uniformly green. Serve or refrigerate in an airtight container for up to 5 days.

USE WITH: Green Goddess Salad Bowls (page 74), grilled or poached salmon (page 228).

ALSO GREAT WITH: Grilled vegetables (especially eggplant, zucchini, onions, or asparagus), blanched vegetables (especially broccoli or cauliflower), roasted vegetables (especially carrot or squash), fried eggs, grilled or roasted chicken, lamb chops, French fries, roasted potatoes, baked potatoes, crudités.

CREAMY PARMESAN DRESSING

MAKES 1 SCANT CUP (ABOUT 240 ML)

Use this dressing the way you use Caesar: to luxuriously coat kale or romaine salads, and give them that satisfying Parmesan finish. Blend (in a blender) for a super-creamy dressing, or whisk together by hand for a chunkier, Parmesan-forward finish. For the Parmesan, use the good stuff. Look for something aged.

½ cup (120 g) mayonnaise

¾ packed cup (25 g) finely grated Parmesan cheese

¼ cup (60 ml) fresh lemon juice

1 Tbsp Dijon mustard

2 tsp Worcestershire sauce

½ to 1 tsp Tabasco sauce

¼ tsp fine sea salt, or to taste

¼ tsp freshly ground black pepper, or to taste

Whisk together the mayonnaise, cheese, lemon juice, mustard, Worcestershire sauce, and Tabasco sauce to taste in a medium bowl until fully combined (it will have some texture, from the cheese). Taste, and add salt and pepper to your liking. Set aside for 20 minutes before serving, or refrigerate in an airtight container for up to 5 days.

USE WITH: The Ravenwood Salad (page 134).

ALSO GREAT WITH: Roast chicken, turkey, grilled mushrooms, French fries, shaved kale and Brussels sprout salad.

Making broth or stock isn't an exact science, and thank goodness—I'd never make it if it were. Instead, it's a flexible, go-with-the-flow formula with delicious rewards: a heady broth to have on hand anytime the urge for soup making arises.

The vegetables below are a guideline; feel free to swap out or add any veggie scraps you may have to flavor the stock, including leeks, celery root, fennel, tomatoes, mushrooms or mushroom stems, and parsnips, aiming to keep the proportions roughly the same as this outline below.

2 Tbsp olive oil

2 onions, coarsely chopped

3 carrots, coarsely chopped

4 stalks celery, coarsely chopped

1 Tbsp red pepper paste (Hungarian, Italian, or Asian)

4 sprigs fresh thyme or 1 bay leaf (or both)

1 small bunch fresh parsley or leftover parsley stems

2 tsp fine sea salt

1 tsp freshly ground black pepper

1 piece of Parmesan cheese rind

Heat the oil in a large pot over medium heat and add all the vegetables. Stir to coat the vegetables, and then add the pepper paste. Stir vigorously over medium heat for 1 minute, until everything is coated. Pour in 12 cups (about 2.8 L) water and add the thyme, parsley, salt, pepper, and cheese rind, and bring to a boil. Lower the heat and simmer until the stock is flavorful and lightly colored, about 1 hour, or longer if you have time. Taste and season with more salt as needed.

Strain, or spoon out the vegetables and herbs with a slotted spoon (and eat them—they're delicious!). Use the stock warm, or let cool completely and divide into airtight containers. Refrigerate for up to 1 week or freeze for 1 month.

USE WITH: Any of the soups in this book, in lieu of chicken broth or stock.

ALSO GREAT WITH: Ramen noodles with cooked vegetables, tofu, poached eggs.

SPICY VEGETABLE STOCK

PREP TIME: **15 MINUTES**

TOTAL TIME: **1 HOUR (OR MORE)**

MAKES **12 CUPS (2.8 L)**

There's not much to say about pickled onions, and then again there is everything to say. They are quick, easy, and an absolute revelation atop soft tacos or pulled pork, sandwiches or tortilla soup, pozole, salads, grain bowls, on a charcuterie spread, and with anything grilled. Make these; you won't regret it.

1 large red onion, thinly sliced

1 garlic clove, halved

½ cup (120 ml) apple cider vinegar

1 tbsp sugar

1 tsp fine sea salt

1 Tbsp olive oil

2 Tbsp finely chopped fresh parsley

Combine the onion, garlic, vinegar, ½ cup (120 ml) water, the sugar, and salt in a pint jar, shake, and set aside at room temperature for 20 minutes. If you plan to use within a day, stir in the oil and parsley. Or refrigerate in an airtight container for up to 2 weeks; stir in the oil and parsley before serving.

USE WITH: Magic Pork Shoulder (page 157), fish tacos (page 146), migas or chilaquiles (page 50), pozole verde (page 82), Hungarian Snacking Tray (page 94), The Everything Lox Lunch (page 98), or Mexican polenta bowls (page 118).

ALSO GREAT WITH: Ground beef tacos, turkey sandwiches, smoked or grilled fish.

GOOD-WITH-EVERYTHING PICKLED ONIONS

PREP TIME: **10 MINUTES**

TOTAL TIME: **30 MINUTES**

SERVES **8**

(makes 1 pint/480 g)

PICKLED WHITE ONIONS AND JALAPEÑO

Use white onions, and add 1 jalapeño, sliced lengthwise, or a single small, dried red chile to the mix. (I use this version with Fish Contramar, page 152.)

PICKLED CARROTS

Combine the above ingredients with 3 large carrots, any color, thinly sliced. Shake and store as above.

SALMON, TWO WAYS

Here's what I learned in culinary school about fish: It should be bought fresh, cooked fresh, and served fresh—as in, right away. Then I learned to cure and cook it in two simple, spectacular ways that require little skill, only patience. Both of these techniques eliminate the two biggest hurdles for cooking fish: flipping fillets whole in a hot pan and mastering perfectly cooked fish for a crowd.

The first method—poaching—is old school, yet akin to the chefy technique sous vide. It yields undeniably tender, un-fishy fillets. The bonus is that you can cook the salmon in advance and store it cooled in the refrigerator, where it stays delicious preserved in oil for at least 1 week, ready for easy flaking and serving. This is also the salmon of choice for the squeamish because there's no odor during cooking.

The second method—curing—yields clean-tasting cold fish that is brilliant sliced thin and served on toast, bagels, and salads, and alongside perfectly scrambled eggs, to name a few options. This salmon is buttery, memorable, and (surprise!) more economical ounce per ounce than those slim commercial packets that disappear in a day.

Why two recipes? Because there's everyday salmon, dinnertime salmon, cold lunch at your desk salmon, Sunday morning breakfast with the paper salmon, and a whole crowd gathered around your kitchen table salmon. These easy recipes yield a little of everything.

OLIVE OIL–POACHED SALMON

PREP TIME: **30 MINUTES**

TOTAL TIME: **1 HOUR**

SERVES **6** (makes 1½ lb/680 g)

1½ lb (680 g) wild salmon, skinned, pin bones removed, cut into 4 fillets

1½ tsp fine sea salt

1 lemon, quartered

1 sprig fresh parsley or thyme

2 garlic cloves, smashed

About 1½ cups (360 ml) extra-virgin olive oil

Season both sides of the salmon with the salt and set aside for 30 minutes.

Meanwhile, bring a large pot of water, big enough to cover a 1 qt (1 L) canning jar by 1 inch (2.5 cm), to a boil over high heat. Have a canning jar with a tight-fitting lid at the ready, and pop the jar into the water to make sure it will be completely submerged.

Pack the pieces of salmon into the jar, add the lemon, parsley, and garlic, and top with oil to cover, within 1 inch (2.5 cm) of the top of the rim, making sure there is oil all around the fish itself. (Don't worry, you won't eat all the oil, but it helps the salmon cook gently, and keeps it moist.) Seal the jar tightly.

Once the water is at a gentle boil, add the jar and immediately remove the pot from the heat. Let the jar sit in the water until the salmon is just cooked through, 20 to 30 minutes. Remove from the water and serve warm, or let cool completely and refrigerate the jar for up to 1 week.

To serve small bits of salmon, bring the jar to room temperature on the counter to let the oil soften. Pull out as much salmon as you plan to use, let it temper on a plate, and serve at room temperature.

To serve all four fillets warm, return the jar to a pot of steaming water and let it sit, off the heat, until the oil in the center of the jar is warm to the touch (to test, insert a knife into the jar halfway, and pull it out. Touch the tip of the knife—it should be warm, but not hot).

HOMEMADE GRAVLAX

PREP TIME: **10 MINUTES**
TOTAL TIME: **2 TO 4 DAYS**
SERVES **16** (makes 1¾ lb/800 g)

1 large bunch fresh dill (40 g), coarsely chopped

¼ cup (40 g) fine sea salt

¼ cup (50 g) sugar

1 Tbsp freshly ground black pepper

6 juniper berries or caraway seeds, crushed (optional)

2 lb (910 g) high-quality fresh salmon fillet (preferably wild), skin on, pin bones removed

cont'd

Combine the dill, salt, sugar, pepper, and juniper berries (if using) in a jar or bowl, and mix together. Line a glass or ceramic baking dish with cheesecloth or plastic wrap, and spread half of the herb mixture evenly over the lined dish. Lay the salmon, skin-side down, onto the herb mixture. Sprinkle on and smooth the remaining herb mixture over the flesh side, making sure every inch of the flesh is well covered.

Wrap the cheesecloth or plastic up around the fish to cover it completely. Wrap the whole dish in plastic wrap, right over the fish, and place a smaller flat baking dish or platter over the length of the fillet. Top with something heavy, like a large can of tomatoes, to keep the salmon weighed down as it cures.

Refrigerate the salmon, turning and draining off the liquid every 1 or 2 days, until the fish is firm, 2 to 4 days, depending on the thickness of the fish. Rewrap as needed throughout the process (usually around the second day).

To finish the curing, remove the fish from the wrap, brush off the entire fillet on both sides very well (a paper towel works for this), and set the fish on a platter to air-dry, uncovered in the refrigerator, for 1 hour.

To serve, slice the fish thinly on a diagonal while cold, leaving the skin behind. Cover any remaining fish well, refrigerate, and use within 1 week. Or wrap any remains tightly in plastic wrap, then aluminum foil. Label and freeze for up to 3 months.

GOOD TO KNOW
Cater the flavor of this fish to your liking with a mishmash of herbs and spices, but keep the salt-sugar ratio the same for best results.

REMOVING PIN BONES
Rub your clean fingers lightly over the salmon fillet to check for pin bones—little almost translucent bones that stick up from the flesh in a pattern down the center of the fillet. Flex the shape of the fillet over your hand so that it curves, flesh side up, and feel for any bumps. Remove any pin bones with tweezers or needle-nose pliers, grasping the top of the bone and gently pulling the bone out, without damaging the flesh. (This gets easier every time, but you can also ask your fishmonger to do this for you.)

WORK SMART, NOT HARD

I love that motto. There's no truer place to apply it than in the kitchen. Every time you make more than you need, and stash some extra aside, you are writing your own destiny for a more satisfying life. Each time you steal a couple of moments away to boil eggs, cut a whole pineapple into chunks, or whiz together a potent green sauce, you give yourself a little boost for your next great meal.

These aren't hard tasks, and if you put on the right podcast and get yourself in the zone, they aren't boring ones, either.

This section is a nod to both helpless and helpful cooks. The helpless will find these little tuck-aways in the refrigerator a lifeline to feeding themselves more successfully. The helpful can use this list as a checklist, and a strategy for building more flavor into their meals.

STRATEGY ONE
Pick one or two tasks from the list below to tackle every time you find yourself with small blocks of time.

STRATEGY TWO
Set aside a block of time every week, and make your own list from the ideas below. Work through it, assigning tasks to any helpers in the house (and don't forget to save time to wrap up and put everything away before you close up shop).

10 minutes

Wash and dry everyday herbs like parsley. Pick the leaves off the stems and store separately, wrapped in damp paper towels, in zipped bags.

Wash, peel, and cut carrots, celery, and peppers. Store, wrapped in damp paper towels, in zipped bags for snacks and soup prep.

Peel and chop fruit for snacks, smoothies, and Vacation Fruit Salad (page 38).

Make chimichurri (page 140) or green sauce (page 220).

Make pickled onions (page 226).

Start the rice cooker for rice porridge (page 46) or grain bowls (page 74).

Make an easy dip (page 90).

Whisk together pancake dry mix (page 30 or 33) and measure and store liquid ingredients (separately). Or do the same with waffles (page 25).

Prepare chia pudding for yogurt bowls (page 20).

Make dressings (page 222).

Start short ribs (page 106) in the slow cooker or oven.

Boil and peel eggs (see page 234) and store in the refrigerator.

20 minutes

Toast nuts (almonds, walnuts), let cool, and store in an airtight container for up to 1 week.

Steam small potatoes or sweet potatoes for grain bowls (page 74).

Make muesli (page 22).

Grill veggies for dinner or grain bowls (page 74).

Make and portion cookie dough (page 179 or 182); refrigerate or freeze.

Make and portion blueberry muffin batter to bake in the morning (page 41).

Prepare and press dough for Easier-than-Pie Warm Apple Tart (It's True) (page 188) into a pan and freeze.

Make and soak strata (page 143) to bake in the morning.

Make The Ravenwood Salad (page 134) and portion into jars for desk/school lunches.

Make (but don't dress) Greek Salad (Sort Of) (page 70).

40 minutes

Cook rice for dinners, lunches, and leftover rice porridge (page 46).

Roast vegetables for dinners and grain bowls (page 74).

Cook whole grains for dinners and grain bowls (page 74).

One hour

Poach chicken (page 126).

Make and roll meatballs (page 109) to freeze for the week.

Make a big pot of pozole (page 82) and refrigerate for the week.

Make Always-On Vegetable Soup (page 78) or Spicy Vegetable Stock (page 225).

Cook beans (see page 235) for polenta bowls (page 118) and taco night (page 146).

Poach salmon (page 228).

Two hours (or a whole afternoon)

Make Sunday Sauce (page 212).

Make Magic Pork Shoulder (page 157).

Bake an Almost-Famous Cranberry Bundt Cake (page 164).

Make banana bread (page 60) or Chocolate Snacking Loaf (page 63).

Make Save-the-Day Spinach Pie (page 215).

Prep and cure Homemade Gravlax (page 229).

PERFECT BOILED EGGS IN UNDER TEN MINUTES

The trick to soft, creamy yolks with tender, set whites is to boil the water first, then add the eggs. Like any method, it requires you sticking close by and watching the water to keep it at a gentle simmer, and removing the eggs not a minute too late. Here's a guide:

runny yolk | 6 to 7 minutes

soft jammy yolk | 7 to 8 minutes

creamy set yolk | 8½ to 9 minutes

hard yolk | 10 minutes

Bring a large pot of water to a rapid boil (about 2 qt/2 L water for 8 eggs). As soon as the water boils, gently lower the eggs in, and keep at a gentle boil. When the timer goes off, immediately remove the eggs from the water and submerge them in a bowl of ice water (or run under very cold water) for 2 whole minutes to stop the cooking; peel and test one egg for doneness before pouring your hot water down the drain.

TWO TEN-MINUTE THINGS TO DO WITH COOKED CHICKEN

AN EASY CHICKEN SALAD

Pick every juicy morsel from the bone; chop 2 packed cups (250 g) cooked chicken (page 126) finely and stir together with 1 finely chopped apple, 1 finely chopped stalk celery, 1 handful minced fresh chives, ½ cup (120 ml) mayo or plain Greek yogurt, 1 teaspoon fresh lemon juice, and ¼ teaspoon each fine sea salt and freshly ground black pepper. Pack in a 1 qt (1 L) container and keep for up to 2 days.

WORLD'S EASIEST BBQ

Add shredded chicken to a pot with a few tablespoons broth per packed cup (125 g) shredded cooked chicken (page 126). Cook over low heat until it breaks down completely, then toss with your favorite barbecue sauce to taste. Layer onto soft potato rolls with mayo and pickles, and serve warm.

GO-TO GRAINS

Grains require little skill, only time. Because the better they are for you, generally speaking, the longer they take to cook, I always throw them into my prep day whenever I have the time. They can bubble away on the stove while vegetables are roasting or you're baking a cake. Simple. By habit, I rinse all my grains once in cold water before cooking, but it's only imperative for quinoa.

Here are my water/stock-to-grain ratios and times. To each, add a generous pinch of salt. The guide below offers rough guidelines for al dente, but take them a touch further if you prefer.

BULGUR

1 cup (160 g) uncooked | 2 cups (480 ml) liquid
Simmer for 15 minutes.

WHITE RICE (LONG-GRAIN)

1 cup (200 g) uncooked | 1½ cups (360 ml) liquid
Simmer for 20 minutes.

RED OR WHITE QUINOA

1 cup (180 g) uncooked | 1¾ cups (420 ml) liquid
Simmer for 15 (for white) to 20 (for red) minutes.

FARRO

1 cup (180 g) uncooked | 3 cups (720 ml) liquid
Simmer for 30 minutes.

BROWN RICE (SHORT-GRAIN)

1 cup (200 g) uncooked | 2 cups (480 ml) liquid
Simmer for 45 minutes.

Toast the grain with a splash of olive oil in a medium saucepan over medium-high heat until just fragrant, 2 to 3 minutes. Add the liquid and a generous pinch of salt, and bring to a boil. Lower the heat and simmer, uncovered (except rice—it cooks best and most evenly when covered tightly)—until the desired tenderness. Drain off any excess water. Remove from the heat, cover, and let steam for 5 minutes. Fluff the grains with a fork before serving.

To store, cool completely in the pan, or spread out on a baking sheet to cool quickly. Transfer to a sturdy zip-top bag or airtight container and store, labeled, in the refrigerator for 2 to 3 days or in the freezer for up to 2 weeks.

QUICK COOKED BEANS

I'm a big fan of a quick canned bean, but weekends are a good excuse to throw on the Instant Pot or pressure cooker and cook a bag of dried beans. Here's how: Rinse 1 pound (455 g) dried beans or chickpeas and pick out any stones. Add to an Instant Pot or stovetop pressure cooker with ½ onion (peeled), 2 garlic cloves (peeled), 2 bay leaves, 1 tablespoon olive oil, 2 teaspoons salt, and 8 cups (2 L) water. Lock the lid and cook on high pressure for 30 minutes (black or pinto beans) or 40 minutes (chickpeas). Turn off the Instant Pot, or remove from the heat, and let the pressure release naturally for 30 minutes. Carefully release the remaining pressure and let the beans cool in the liquid. Serve or store (I like to keep the flavorful liquid, and spoon off as desired), labeled, in the refrigerator for 3 to 4 days or in the freezer for up to 2 months.

ROASTING DAY!

In our house, Roasting Day is a day to cele-brate. Though my family doesn't always know it's happening (I roast, ferociously, while my kids are out playing, not in the line of fire of hot baking sheets), they will certainly know come dinnertime that I've given every vegeta-ble in the house the love.

Since I almost never turn on the oven to roast or cook just one thing (truly: never), Roasting Day can come any day my oven is already on, say, to bake a batch of muffins or roast a whole bird. While it's hot, every last edible vegetable in the refrigerator gets roasted, too. Some things mix and match easily on one baking sheet—with relatively similar baking times. Others need their own baking sheet. Some days (winter days, particularly), there are five or six, plus any available casserole dish, lined up with cut vegetables doused in olive oil and salt, waiting for a turn.

You can add an herb, a few cloves of garlic, or a slice or two of lemon if you have them on hand, but I often keep Roasting Day simple and straight up: good olive oil (one whose flavor I like all on its own), flaky sea salt, and freshly ground pepper is all most vegetables need to rise to their potential.

LOVE YOUR SHEET PAN
Whatever you're doing in the kitchen—peeling vegetables, slicing bread, peeling hard-boiled eggs— work over a rimmed sheet pan or baking sheet. Let your extras fall onto the pan, and swipe it into the garbage or compost with one fell swoop—easy cleanup!

EASY ROAST VEGETABLES

2 lb (910 g) vegetables, cut into bite-size pieces
Several garlic cloves (optional)
¼ cup (60 ml) olive oil
Fine sea salt
Freshly ground black pepper
2 to 3 sprigs fresh thyme or rosemary (optional)

Preheat the oven to 425°F (220°C).

Toss the vegetables and garlic (if using) with the oil in a large bowl, and season with salt, pepper, and herbs (if using). Spread the mixture on a baking sheet and roast until they are browned and tender when pierced with a fork, 45 minutes to 1 hour, depending on the vegetable. Give the pan a good shake halfway through the cooking, after about 20 minutes, to turn the vegetables around for even cooking.

CALLING ALL CAULIFLOWER LOVERS AND HATERS
If you already know the virtues of roasted cauliflower, you know how amazing a heavy sprinkling of finely grated Parmesan cheese added to the last 10 minutes of baking will be. Try it. If you think cauliflower is not your veggie, make this easy, addictive dish (adding 3 to 4 tablespoons grated Parm at the end) to find out if you might be wrong. All bets that you can't resist it. Be generous with the cheese, and you'll also get golden Parmesan crisps (aka frico) anywhere it has fallen that peel off the pan into addictive crispy bits.

IMPROMPTU MAGIC

There are many stories about how I started cooking, but the one my dad tells is this: In high school, while my classmates were buzzing across town for lunch at Taco Bell, my gang would head to my house instead (less rushing, more eating; it's always been my thing). My parents say no matter how sure they were there was *nothing* in the house to eat, I would open the refrigerator, pull out a handful of random ingredients, and concoct a fast, filling lunch. At its worst, it was healthier than Taco Bell, and at least good enough that my friends came back again the next day. At best, we ate like kings.

This—impromptu cooking—is what I most wish to pass along. I want you to open your refrigerator and see not a bunch of random ingredients, but your next promising meal. Some of those ingredients may take some flexing and love, yes, but most of them can add up to something that feels like a little win—even if it's not the sexiest meal you've had all week.

Because no matter how carefully I plan or shop, by the end of the week our refrigerator holds little more than mustard and maple syrup, a few scraps of herbs and cheese, and the yellowing kale from our week's CSA. It's nearly impossible to gauge exactly how much it will take to feed a family, or even yourself, from day to day. Life is unpredictable. Before you toss the scraps straight in the compost bin, visit this list. When I do—whenever I lean on impromptu magic—I'm always glad I did.

STRATEGY ONE:
Scan your refrigerator for usable little bits, and note what you have the most of. Visit this list for inspiration to resurrect your extras—and save a few coins, too—before shop day rolls around again.

STRATEGY TWO:
Intentionally put aside small bits from your favorite meals, with a future refrigerator cleanout in mind. Plan on working these lists toward the end of every week.

Things to Make with Vegetable Bits (Root Vegetables, Peppers, Squash)

The rules: Mix and match. Wash and peel root vegetables, and if they're really tragic, soak them in ice water (which instantly adds new life to limp vegetables). Chop into small bits and toss into salads (see the Greek salad on page 70), or cook gently in a little oil, with salt, pepper, and your favorite herbs or spices, and use in/with:

Omelets

Tacos

Grain or rice bowls with egg and veggies

Always-On Vegetable Soup (page 78)

Rice bowl with a fried egg (bibimbap)

Scrambled eggs and veggies
(see migas, page 50)

Things to Make with Berries and Other Fruit Bits

The rules: Wash thoroughly, and trim any bruised or off bits from whole fruit; chop. Toss any moldy berries. Mix and match berries and other fruits, and freeze if you can't use them right away or keep separately in the refrigerator to top/stir/blend/add into:

Muesli (page 22)

Smoothies (page 208)

Eton Mess (page 194)

Blueberry muffins (page 41), mixed leftover berries

Ice cream or pancakes (toss with honey or maple syrup)

Toasted bread with ricotta and mashed berries; drizzle with honey

Things to Make with Citrus Bits

The rules: Wash thoroughly and trim any bruised or moldy bits. Zest and juice any remaining mostly wholes or halves and save for:

Chimichurri (page 140), Spicy Tomatillo-Lime Sauce (page 146), and green sauce (page 220)

Vacation Fruit Salad (page 38)

Everyday Dressings (page 222)

Things to Make with Herb Bits

The rules: Pull away any super-wilted or fuzzy parts (anything moldy goes). Wash bright and lively parts and pick off the stems. Chop and add to:

Green sauce (page 220) or chimichurri (page 140)

Grain and greens bowls (page 74)

Green smoothies (page 209) (best with parsley, mint, or cilantro)

Herb omelets

Fried rice

Things to Make with Bits of Greens

The rules: Compost or pitch any pre-washed greens that are stinky, slimy, or past their expiration date. For heads of lettuce, peel away any brown or wilted leaves. Toss any brown or yellow hearty greens like kale or collards. Thinly slice larger leaves to add to:

Grain and greens bowls (page 74)

Green smoothie (page 209; best with kale or spinach)

Scrambled eggs with avocado and greens (page 36)

Risotto (best with kale, spinach, or romaine) (page 120)

The Ravenwood Salad (page 134; best with romaine, kale, radicchio, or cabbage)

Summer Macaroni (Not Just for Summer) (page 114; best with kale or spinach)

Sandwiches

Things to Make with Cheese Bits

The rules: Lob off anything dried or moldy and trim away any rinds, so everything is clean and easy for melting. (Here's a good rule of thumb: small mold bits can be trimmed off hard or semi-hard cheeses, like Parmesan, Gruyère, or Cheddar; mold on soft cheese like goat cheese, ricotta, or triple-crèmes mean the whole lot needs to go.) Chop into cubes or shred to make into:

Summer Macaroni (Not Just for Summer) (page 114)

Cheese and veggie omelets

Quesadillas

Grilled cheese sandwiches

Strata (page 143)

Things to Make with Meat Bits

The rules: Most leftover meats taste better and go further when shredded. Shred chicken, pork, or short rib with forks; moisten with a splash of warm broth or water and a drizzle of oil over low heat. Top/add to:

Sunday Sauce (page 212)

Quick pork, chicken, or beef fried rice

Loaded mostly vegetable and a little meat soup (page 78)

Risotto (page 120)

Enchiladas with Spicy Tomatillo-Lime Sauce (page 146)

Things to Make with Dairy Bits

The rules: Toss anything expired, moldy, curdled, or off-smelling (no, you can't skim the mold off yogurt or sour cream and use the rest). Use the remaining small bits in baked goods. If the recipe calls for half-and-half: mix remaining milk plus cream to equal the total cup yield. If the recipe calls for buttermilk: combine equal parts milk and yogurt or sour cream to equal the total cup yield. Use to make:

French toast

Bread pudding

Rice pudding (page 192)

Strata (page 143)

Muffins (page 41)

Pancakes (page 33)

Decadent hot chocolate

Chocolate pudding

Things to Make with Grain Bits

The rules: Smell—old or expired cooked grains have an immediate funk; toss them. If fresh, combine different grains (think rice, quinoa, farro) to make a larger quantity to use in:

Brown rice porridge (page 46)

Grain and greens bowls (page 74)

SOURCES

FOOD AND SUSTAINABILITY

Outside your own garden, the best source for produce is usually your local farmers' market. Here's where to find the markets and CSAs that sell local organic harvest nearest to your zip code.

Local Harvest
www.localharvest.org

Issues around sustainability change frequently; these resources offer news and updates regularly.

Marine Stewardship Council
www.msc.org

Monterey Bay Aquarium Seafood Watch
www.montereybayaquarium.org

Sustainable Table
www.sustainabletable.org

GIVING

If your table has been blessed with plenty, considering using these recipes and menus as inspiration to give back. Here are some organizations that are making it easy for you to get involved.

City Harvest
www.cityharvest.org

The Edible Schoolyard Project
https://edibleschoolyard.org

FEED
www.feedprojects.com

No Kid Hungry
www.nokidhungry.com

CHEESE, OILS, AND OLIVES

Artisanal Premium Cheese
www.artisanalcheese.com

Murray's Cheese
www.murrayscheese.com

Saxelby Cheesemongers
https://saxelbycheese.com

CHOCOLATE

Callebaut
www.callebaut.com

Scharffen Berger
www.scharffenberger.com

Valrhona
www.valrhona-chocolate.com

GRAINS + SPECIALTY FLOURS

Anson Mills
www.ansonmills.com

Arrowhead Mills
www.arrowheadmills.com

Bob's Red Mill
www.bobsredmill.com

King Arthur Flour
www.kingarthurflour.com

INTERNATIONAL INGREDIENTS

Asian Food Grocer
www.asianfoodgrocer.com

Otto's European and Hungarian Import Store & Deli
www.hungariandeli.com

SALTS + BITTERS

The Meadow
https://themeadow.com

SPICES + VANILLA

Kalustyan's
https://foodsofnations.com

Penzeys Spices
www.penzeys.com

The Spice House
www.thespicehouse.com

CERAMICS

Henry Street Studio
https://henrystreetstudio.com

Herriott Grace
https://herriottgrace.com

LAIL Design
www.laildesign.net

DISHWARE, COOKWARE + BAKING TOOLS

Crate & Barrel
www.crateandbarrel.com

Le Creuset
wwww.lecreuset.com

Field Company
https://fieldcompany.com

JB Prince
www.jbprince.com

Kitchenaid
www.kitchenaid.com

Lodge
www.lodgemfg.com

Staub
www.staubusa.com

Sur La Table
www.surlatable.com

Terrain
www.shopterrain.com

Vitamix
www.vitamix.com

West Elm
www.westelm.com

Williams-Sonoma
www.williams-sonoma.com